WHAT YOUR TEAM WON'T TELL YOU

WHAT YOUR TEAM WON'T TELL YOU

THE 7 MANAGEMENT FAILS TO AVOID

TANYA UYIGUE

Berrett-Koehler
PUBLISHERS

Berrett-Koehler Publishers, Inc.
1333 Broadway, Suite P100
Oakland, CA 94612-1921
(510) 817-2277
bkconnection.com

Ordering Information
Quantity sales. Special discounts are available on quantity purchases by corporations, associations, individuals, and others. For details, please go to bkconnection.com to see our bulk discounts or contact bookorders@bkpub.com for more information.
Textbook exam/desk copies. Please consult the General FAQ at bkconnection.com.
Bookstore orders for trade or textbook use. For print books, please contact Penguin Random House Publisher Services at customerservice@penguinrandomhouse.com. For ebooks, contact your favorite distributor.

Distributed to the US trade and internationally by Penguin Random House Publisher Services.

The authorized representative in the EU for product safety and compliance is EU Compliance Partner, Pärnu mnt. 139b-14, 11317 Tallinn, Estonia, www.eucompliancepartner.com, +372 5368 65 02.

Printed in The United States of America

Berrett-Koehler books are printed on long-lasting acid-free paper. When it is available, we choose paper that has been manufactured by environmentally responsible processes. These may include using trees grown in sustainable forests, incorporating recycled paper, minimizing chlorine in bleaching, or recycling the energy produced at the paper mill.

Library of Congress Cataloging-in-Publication Data
Names: Uyigue, Tanya author
Title: What your team won't tell you : the 7 management fails to avoid / Tanya Uyigue.
Other titles: What your team will not tell you
Description: First edition. | Oakland, CA : Berrett-Koehler Publishers, Inc, [2026] | Includes index.
Identifiers: LCCN 2026008247 (print) | LCCN 2026008248 (ebook) | ISBN 9798890571960 paperback | ISBN 9798890571977 pdf | ISBN 9798890571984 epub
Subjects: LCSH: Industrial management | Leadership
Classification: LCC HD31.2 .U97 2026 (print) | LCC HD31.2 (ebook)
LC record available at https://lccn.loc.gov/2026008247
LC ebook record available at https://lccn.loc.gov/2026008248

First Edition
35 34 33 32 31 30 29 28 27 26 10 9 8 7 6 5 4 3 2 1

Book production: Happenstance Type-O-Rama
Cover design: Ashley Ingram
Cover image: Generated with OpenArt AI

For those who've shared their truth,
and the leaders who modeled
what was possible

CONTENTS

PREFACE
GET COMFORTABLE BEING UNCOMFORTABLE

Writing this was much harder than I thought it would be because I knew that the things I wanted to say, and the way I wanted to say them, weren't going to sit well with everyone. You, as a manager, may feel offended or defensive. But I'm tired. I'm tired of having to be so careful with my words when giving feedback or just stating my experience and how I feel.

Where can we speak freely? If the only places we can say how we *really* feel are at home or when we're out with friends, how will anything ever change? Where can we critique the workplace and the leadership in these companies without having to tiptoe around your feelings?

The point of this book is to help managers like you see the impact of a leadership style you may not even realize is harmful. In many companies and on many teams, you can't critique a manager without consequence. It happens often: People gasp or give a look to a favorite colleague when someone questions something a manager did that was unfair, unrealistic, or problematic for the staff. People quietly exchange looks or send side texts to say, "Did you see what they said?"

Most of the time, the questions or concerns presented were on everyone's minds. They are fair critiques. That staff person is the brave one (or sometimes just the naive one who doesn't realize they've put a target on their back for questioning the way it is!). The unspoken rule at work is that criticism is only acceptable flowing in one direction—from top down.

I want this book to be a safe space for both you, as a manager, and the people you manage. When I share content online and people say, "I wish I could send this to my manager," I'm always tempted to say, "Send me their email address!" So, think of this book as my email to you!

Now, I know if you're a manager reading this right now, you might be thinking, "I DO take a beating at work. Management sucks. All I get is disrespect and nothing but complaints about the kind of manager I am or am not." I promise you, some people are still holding back. They don't hate you; they just don't respect the way you choose to lead. They believe it's to their benefit and a form of survival to endure, because bills need to be paid and you won't listen anyway. They see how you respond to others who push back even a little bit, so they don't think it's worth it to push at all. Instead, they roll with things. They'll go to happy hours, laugh at the jokes, and ask about your weekend. It's part of "work."

But they can't tell you everything.

How controlling you are, how jealous you seem, how uninterested you are.

They won't tell you how they just wish you would relax because they don't want your job, especially since you sure don't seem so happy in the role.

They won't tell you that they're not trying to outshine you. They're just talented and skilled and shouldn't have to hide that.

They won't tell you they want more direction and acknowledgment, and they want you to check in on their progress and work because they have goals too—it's not all about you.

It's just not safe to tell you these things. On their behalf, I'm going to tell you a lot.

For managers, it is safe for you to read this book and reflect a bit—maybe a lot!

This book isn't for every manager; it's for people in management who are open, curious, and willing to reflect. You're ready to be uncomfortable if it leads to growth. If you're curious about whether your existing approach to your team may need some adjustments or a complete overhaul, this is the book for you. If you've noticed engagement on your team has gone down, that's not entirely on you, but as a manager, you have an impact. When looking back on my career, when revisiting conversations with colleagues, when recalling coaching conversations with clients, one thing is clear: The way people experience culture at their company is often through their manager. The relationship between you and your direct reports means something. Every interaction with you is impactful. Different teams at a company can have totally different experiences, as can different people on your team.

This book explores seven management styles that can get in the way of having an engaged staff with whom you have a healthy working relationship. In some cases, these are things you may do a little bit without realizing how much of an impact they have on the people around you. You'll be able to reflect on some of these patterns and hear from countless people who have shared with me challenging work experiences that have impacted how they feel and perform, not only at work but in their lives away from it. You'll gain some understanding of why you may engage with your team the way you do and explore how to take a different approach.

You don't have to tell anyone that you read this book or how many items you checked off in the chapter assessments. You don't need to tell anyone if you identify with any of the archetypes mentioned; that's your business.

You don't have to share your fears or insecurities with anyone, but seeing them in written form can be powerful. I hope you can be open to the possibility that you haven't led in the way you wanted, or in a way that was of your own design. Sometimes we just repeat the cycle from our mentors or previous managers, pushing down our own values and pushing through feelings of guilt or even sadness because we know things aren't right but don't know what else to do.

Being a manager who does something different, especially in toxic spaces, puts a target on you.

Will you challenge the status quo at your company? Will you advocate for your staff and yourself? How many more years do you want to spend afraid in your role?

You have to decide whether you want to be brave like the people on your staff who ask hard questions and put you on the spot. Sometimes they are truly annoying people who have it out for you, and other times they are just curious, smart, and courageous. Both can show you how leadership can be uncomfortable. I've found that uncomfortable stuff is what makes us grow and get better. **Get comfortable being**

uncomfortable while you read this book. In the last chapter, you'll get a chance to make some choices that allow you to move forward in a way that's authentic to who you are, how you want to feel, and the type of experience you'd like the people around you to have.

I've worked for a lot of people. They were each powerful in their own way. They had the titles and the ability to get themselves from one rung on the ladder to the next. I don't have too many fond memories of all of them. The ones I admired the most were the people who weren't just trying to grow themselves; they tried to help bring me up too—or they told me it was OK for me to grow out, because they knew the company didn't respect or nurture talent like mine. These were the leaders who took the time to connect with me. They weren't just digging for information about my personal life, trying to fake a friendship. They sought to understand what my professional goals were, what my values were, and what motivated me. The level of support I got from these leaders is what everyone should have. Not support rooted in favoritism, but in respect for the contributions I made, my transparency, and my consistency. These are the leaders who have inspired me, from my first internships out of college to those who supported me while I was on their team, writing this book.

The good news for managers is that no matter how much of a micromanager or gatekeeper you are, there are staff who are still willing to try. They don't give you a hard time, they don't talk about you too much behind your back, and they have compassion for you. These people go to work every day and fight the good fight, despite how they are led. They see the bigger picture and can show you a model of healthy leadership. Unfortunately, these same employees are eventually going to get tired of having to fight each day. Giving you the benefit of the doubt, constantly seeing things from your perspective, and overlooking the mess will get old. They will leave, and the company will suffer for it.

As a manager, you are in the best position to lead through some much-needed change. You have influence, you can inspire, you can mentor and coach. You can create a model of the type of environment people can thrive in.

WHAT YOUR TEAM WON'T TELL YOU

INTRODUCTION
HOW TO USE THIS BOOK

How you approach this book is up to you. You can read it straight through from beginning to end, or you can skip to the archetype chapter(s) that you believe may align with your current management style. It's possible that you may align, even on a small level, with an archetype you weren't aware of, so reading those chapters could help you become more self-aware. You may know for sure that a particular archetype is far removed from your management approach, but you may still find value in learning more about why your former manager—or even a colleague—led that way. There is no wrong way to do this. What's important is to be open and honest with yourself.

I chose the seven archetypes in this book based on common challenges people have shared with me when discussing their relationships with their managers. The archetypes represent management styles that consistently impact culture, engagement, and trust in the workplace. When I am coaching and creating content, these archetypes and patterns of behavior often come up for people from all walks of life. So often people share, This is what my manager does; this is how I feel—what do I do?

Each chapter will address one of seven archetypal manager fails:

THE MICROMANAGER / CONTROL FREAK Hovers over their staff

THE ABSENTEE MANAGER / GHOST Avoids much contact with their staff

THE SPOTLIGHT SEEKER / CREDIT STEALER Takes credit for the work of others

THE GATEKEEPER / BLOCKER Blocks people from growing beyond their current position

THE BURNOUT CREATOR / MARTYR Models unhealthy approaches to work

THE CULTURE ENFORCER / MOLD MAKER Values conformity over performance

THE TOXIC OPTIMIST / PRETENDER Avoids being honest about workplace realities

You'll notice a consistent structure in each archetype chapter. A self-assessment at the beginning will give you the opportunity to reflect on your behaviors and certain tendencies. The self-assessments and alignment ranges are a starting point, not a final verdict. They aren't meant to diagnose you or put you in a box. They're a way to help you slow down, notice patterns, and reflect on how these feelings, thoughts, and actions show up for you, especially when you're under stress. I'll then provide a detailed description of the archetype to increase understanding beyond the assessment. I have personal stories to share, as well as information about what may cause managers to think, feel, and act the way they do.

For years, in coaching sessions, I have created space for hundreds of people to share with me how they experience their workplace and their manager. In each chapter, I have included their collective experiences set in two distinct voices. Each highlights different responses to the stress of reporting to the archetype. One voice represents the sadness and self-doubt of an employee under that manager, while the other voice represents the anger and resentment of a different employee under that same manager. Additionally, I include real quotes pulled directly from my social media content that align with people's experiences of different archetypes.

At the end of each chapter, you'll see tips and real actions you can take to make a shift. You'll be able to decide whether any changes in your approach are necessary. If you're willing to reflect on some of your tendencies and patterns, especially in environments where you are stressed, feel like you're fighting for your survival, or are just struggling with your confidence, you can get a lot out of reading this. This isn't about your personality type; these archetypes are descriptions of what you do, not who you are as a person.

A note on discomfort: Reading the social media quotes and employee voices, reflecting on the assessment statements, and reading the patterns described in the chapters may cause you to feel a range of emotions. Anger, frustration, and defensiveness—sometimes even embarrassment or guilt. This is normal! As a manager, you also may align and agree with some of what you read because you're an employee too. You work in the same system as everyone else.

When moments come up where you feel uncomfortable, **pause**. Take that time to get curious about why something you are reading stirs something up within you. Do you disagree with the description of a particular archetype? Do you disagree that the patterns aligned with any archetype are even something to be concerned about? Do any of the employee quotes or voices remind you of staff you've had and didn't particularly like? Does the tone of the book bother you? When you disagree with something, take note of it. Write down what you would say or what you think instead.

You don't need to agree with everything in this book for it to be useful. Not everyone will see themselves in every archetype. Pay attention to places where you have reactions, resist, or keep going back to something. That's where valuable information lives.

Don't beat yourself up for anything you've said or done in the past as a manager. This book is meant to help us all build more awareness. That awareness will get you closer to choosing what you'd like to do moving forward, armed with so much more information than before you read this book. There's no rush! Changes take time, and the sections at the end of the chapter that include suggested shifts aren't meant to be done in any particular order, nor overnight, and not necessarily on your own. Any shift in the way you engage with your staff, any shift in the way you think and feel about yourself, is worthwhile. Those shifts, whether big or small, can have a huge impact not only on your experience as a manager but on the ways your staff and others experience you.

1

How Patterns Form

The toughest, most infuriating moment of my career was something that many people have experienced. I applied for a promotion and didn't get it. That experience led me to become a coach, create content, and write this book.

When I started creating content on social media, I avoided telling that story. My content, while informed by my experiences and observations from having had so many different types of jobs, wasn't about me specifically. One day I decided I wanted to get more personal, not because I wanted to call anyone out, but because I wanted my supporters to know I wasn't yet another grifting online coach who had little experience and couldn't relate to what people were going through. **I get what people are going through, because I have been, and am, one of them!** I've been burned at work. I've messed up. I've been overlooked. I've been a bad manager, and I've been a great one. I've been a superstar individual contributor, and I've been what folks call a "quiet quitter."

Sharing my story online was tough because I'm the coach—I'm here to listen to you. During my coach training, they drilled into us that it's not about you; it's always about them. Social media is a bit different, so I recorded my story and sat on it for about a month. I thought it was too long (three whole minutes) and too personal. I didn't want people to think I was a bitter, angry Black woman who didn't get something she wanted at work and had to let the world know. The thinking may be that hiring managers don't make mistakes. As someone who has been a hiring manager, I can say we definitely do!

The response to the video was overwhelming because my story wasn't unique. I had spent years at a company being a very loyal employee. I was the above and beyond type. I applied for a more senior role because I believed I had earned it and knew I could do it well and have a great impact. I didn't get the role, and an external hire was made. The external hire lasted about sixty days before the company decided that person wasn't the right fit. No, they didn't circle back to me, but they did promote one of my colleagues whom I had helped hire in the years prior. So, someone I hired became my boss—fun stuff!

I never learned why I wasn't promoted. When I asked, I was told how magnificent the external candidate was. I was told directly by the hiring manager that I was qualified and would do well, but they "couldn't pass up" this person. I felt cheated again, this time not just out of the opportunity, but out of getting real feedback. I felt erased after years of dedicating my time, energy, and creativity to that company. In the end, I wasn't even worth an explanation. I couldn't even get a tip or two on what to do that would make me someone they "couldn't pass up"? I didn't like that leadership didn't have to take any accountability or give me clear feedback, that there was no commitment to growth, and that they lacked the courage to have real conversations with me.

In the next couple of years after that experience, I replayed everything about it and my entire time at the company in my mind. I saw a lot about myself that I didn't like. I had gotten comfortable. I ignored my gut. My experience toward the end was a messy series of failures. Not just on leadership, but on me. I played myself while they played me. I started thinking beyond that job and reflecting on the leadership failures that took place throughout my career with numerous previous managers, and with myself as a manager.

I took to social media to share all types of information about the workplace, including what to pay attention to within yourself, the company, and the person you report to. Content about toxic leadership is often a hit. I noticed comments and follows from people of all backgrounds, in all types of industries, describing similar experiences with managers. People were not just venting or talking about a few bad apples. It was clear that some leadership behaviors were making people feel like they couldn't go to work and thrive. It doesn't have to be this way. Managers are powerful and can have the most positive impact on their staff. A great manager is like a great teacher; you will never forget them and will tell stories about them decades later. You may choose to go into management because you want to be for someone else what your managers were to you. I am beyond thankful for the inspiring, encouraging, and transparent managers I've had. They are models for the type of leader I strive to be.

This book isn't meant to bash managers as always being the problem. We all contribute to the culture at work, and anyone can bring toxicity into an environment. Some people are a headache to lead. You're not always the problem, but you almost always hold more power. Due to power dynamics, you can criticize your staff in ways they can't criticize you in return without consequences, including retaliation. We tell people it's OK to give feedback to leadership at work, if they say it nicely. The reality is, it doesn't matter how nicely you say anything; it's a tough thing to give feedback to your own boss. I've heard "I wish I could send this to my boss" enough times in my comments section and DMs. So, I'm sharing feedback with you here in the hope that you'll see a part of yourself and commit to trying a different approach.

This is not just about helping your current and future staff have a better experience; this is also for your own benefit. Everyone has different reasons for going into management, but once you get there, you typically want to excel, which means your team should excel. When you disrespect, ignore, or minimize your high performers, or anyone on your team, you lose them. There are certain types of employees you can't afford to keep losing. They bring ideas and get stuff done. If they are respected and well liked by colleagues, they bring good vibes, and you don't want to lose that energy. What I've seen happen numerous times is once you lose one or two of these folks, others follow. You can try to explain away your poor retention for a while, but eventually it will be clear who the common denominator is.

When I went through my promotion experience, someone said, "If they'll do that to her, what will they do to us?" People do watch how you treat others; they see who and what is valued and decide if that aligns with their own values. It can take a while, but losing the respect of your staff because of how you treat people, whether they are high performers or not, is something to be concerned about. Trust is tough in the workplace, but it's a beautiful thing and a necessary thing if you want people to buy into whatever you're selling. After layoffs at a company, one of my colleagues told me, "I'll never believe anything they say here again."

None of this happens overnight. It takes time for people to recognize what's going on, what kind of leader you are, and to decide how they respond. The people who quit are one thing, but those who stay on your payroll and disengage? That can be the most brutal. You can't easily get rid of people, and it's a huge effort to try to reverse the damage.

While reading about the different manager archetypes, keep in mind some of the common threads, what is at the root of the way these managers think and feel, and how that leads to the things they do. You will see a common thread of a stressful type of energy that includes insecurity, fear, and a need for control and comfort.

ENERGY

When I use the word *energy*, I'm referring to your overall vibe as a leader. We all bring our own vibe and style to our leadership approach; this is what makes us unique. Our vibe is informed by our experiences, our training, our beliefs, our emotions, and more. If you see yourself reflected in one or more of these archetypes, ask yourself, "Is this my approach because it's a habit, my go-to, or intentional?"

Reactive energy, in simple terms, is stress. It's limiting and brings you down. When in this state, you can't quite see what your options are; all you can see is that there's a problem. You view the problem as something within yourself, or something within others. It can keep you and even some of the people around you from thriving. It sounds one hundred percent negative, but I think there can be benefits to this energy at times. Some of the emotions we associate with reactive energy include sadness, anger, and frustration. As a person who is typically viewed as strong and put together, by showing a little hurt, I could encourage someone to finally reach out and help me! Anger sometimes pushes me—and many of you—into action. So, these "negative" emotions, in my opinion, can be useful, but we need to understand that they aren't sustainable.

You will read examples of reactive energy and emotions throughout this book and feel them yourself. Things like embarrassment, guilt, apathy, blame. You may see them in an archetype description that feels familiar to you. You will see them in the employee responses. You may even feel some of these emotions toward me for writing about them. Some examples of reactive language and phrases that you might have heard, thought, or said yourself include "Good help is hard to find" and "These people will never change."

It's OK. We all experience these types of thoughts at some point. As leaders, we have to be careful because if this is the vibe we experience and project more often than not, it can cause a lot of problems within our work and on our teams. Even if you do get the results you desire from your team, there will be a lot more complaints, gossip, and burnout along the way.

We don't want to always be in a state of frustration or resentment, so this is where as leaders, we want to lean more toward being intentional about how we think, feel, and ultimately what we do. We don't want to show up to work and let our staff, our leadership, or the work itself control our vibe that day. Making the choice is a powerful type of leadership and, admittedly, not easy.

We can choose to live and lead with a less stressful vibe more often than not. The less stressful vibe is called intentional energy, and it can feel better to both us and those around us. Shifting to these intentional vibes can help everyone be more productive. Instead of bringing you down, this builds you up. Instead of seeing problems, you see possibilities and solutions. Some examples of intentional emotions include calm, clarity, and confidence. Some examples of intentional language and phrases that you may have heard, thought, or said yourself include "How you feel is valid" and "How can I help you?"

Our vibe can be contagious. In each archetype chapter, I included stories about how employees experienced that archetype. Their stories will show you how some employees internalize their experiences with you.

As you read the employee stories in this book, take the opportunity to reflect and pay attention. Do they sound or feel familiar? What might you be doing to contribute to the different emotions of your staff? Have you ever unintentionally brought a vibe that might have influenced the conditions your staff was working in? Do the voices in these chapters reflect the type of culture you want to be a part of or create?

Everyone is responsible for their own feelings, thoughts, and behaviors, but as a leader, you get to be influential. Being proactive, honest, and validating are all things that can help your staff keep going, even when they don't want to. You have the power to set the tone without being phony or smiling through the mess. They feel your vibes and want to experience that too!

SAFE BETS

So much of poor leadership comes from that stressful energy, which is why people feel insecure, fearful, and uncomfortable with themselves and ultimately uncomfortable with those around them whom they compare themselves to and compete with. A way managers try to manage or limit their discomfort is by surrounding themselves with safe bets.

Looking for and wanting to surround yourself with "safe bet" employees is what lies beneath so much of the dysfunctional behavior of poor managers. Across all of these archetypes exists a thread of wanting people to do exactly what you say, not get in your way, not outshine you, stay silent when you misbehave, mimic your level of hustle without question, fit securely into the leadership box you create, and smile through all the mess. Who are these safe bet employees that make you feel so comfortable? The ones you pick for promotions, the ones you hire, the ones you like to keep close?

Safe bet employees are predictable. You know what they are going to do or say in any situation. They are nonthreatening to you. These safe bets have palatable personalities. As an introverted Black person, this one really gets under my skin because it requires so much energy to try to make people feel comfortable with you and safe around you. You have to reassure people that you're not mean or mad; you're just quiet and observant. We may not be great with small talk, forced smiles, or other performative acts, but overall, we're good.

These employees are like mirrors for you. This isn't just about how people look, though in some cases, I wouldn't discount that. It's more that you prefer your staff to be culturally aligned. You want those who make decisions the way you make decisions. The ones who influence the way you influence. If you're extroverted and have staff who are introverted, it can be hard for some of you to see yourselves in them. If you're data driven and have folks on your staff who are led by their intuition, you may struggle to see them as culturally aligned. You want the low maintenance employees. For you Absentee Managers, you love employees who don't need check-ins or too much in regard to accommodations. You want the staff who are adaptable and can move forward through all the chaos.

You want people who won't ever call things out and who tiptoe around letting you know when something is very wrong because you are too fragile to take direct feedback. They won't quit on you either. They seem loyal and, in some cases, willing to sacrifice aspects of their personal lives for the company and the job. They are focused on you, your goals, and staying out of the way.

You might be wondering, What's so wrong with wanting employees like this? It's hard enough to lead; why would we want any trouble? You're not wrong about some of the skills and traits—they can be great to have. However, the way managers want these skills and traits packaged within their staff doesn't set you up for success. You end up with a team of scared, uninspired "yes" people who don't help you grow as a leader or a person. While that may give you a sense of peace at times, this preference for safe bets highlights your need for control, your desire to be comfortable, and shows how much you lead from fear.

INSECURITY AND FEAR

Insecurity is at the root of many leadership failures. We can all be insecure at various points in our life, but when you're in a position to lead people, insecurity can bring out some dark behaviors in even well-intentioned individuals. I personally have experienced this and went through a wave of emotions across several years, as it's an experience you never forget and can't always easily just get over.

Insecurity doesn't always look like fear, but it's present. This is undoubtedly the case for most, if not all, of the archetypes. What's most important for you to know is that the insecurity isn't loud, but it's right there. This is what causes you to perform instead of lead and to view many things and people as threats instead of opportunities. Your ability to recognize and acknowledge your own insecurity will be required for you to become a more effective leader.

Come to each chapter with an open mind and a willingness to try something new. You aren't a villain, and this isn't a book to bash you—it's to call out behaviors that are harmful, whether you are aware of them or not. It's to help prevent you from becoming the very person you once complained about at work. One of the hardest things for me when I transitioned from individual contributor to manager was seeing where I was not as effective, not as strong. When you're new to this type of role, you start to see you're not just managing a team and tasks; you also have to manage your relationships with your own managers. Your direct reports and managers may have different goals or very different views on how to achieve them in a way that acknowledges everyone's time, energy, and needs. It's easy to feel pushed, pulled, and stuck in the middle.

I've seen what happens when companies fall apart. I've been in spaces where everything started out great and then went downhill as leadership weakened. Leadership forgot that without a healthy staff that feels acknowledged, included, and able to grow, you have nothing. It doesn't matter what your product or service is; your employees are the first group of people you need to serve. No, you can't please everyone, but you would be surprised how little people are asking for and how easy it is to deliver. In this book, you'll see how much of an impact you have on people's well-being during their time with you and how it impacts them when they're not at work. Once you have that information, you will get to choose what type of leader you want to be.

2

The Micromanager / Control Freak

IS THIS YOU?

- ☐ I'm not a Micromanager; I just care a lot about the work and our outcomes.
- ☐ I believe if I want something done right, I need to do it myself.
- ☐ Step-by-step instructions ensure things are done correctly.
- ☐ People need to earn my trust before I give them freedom here.
- ☐ I like being copied on emails because it keeps me in the loop.
- ☐ It makes me uncomfortable to not know what people are working on at all times.
- ☐ I'll get blamed if my team makes mistakes, and that threatens my credibility.

- ☐ People will slack off if I don't give them constant direction and attention.
- ☐ It's frustrating when people don't do things the way I do them.
- ☐ I usually revise my staff's work before it goes out.

8–10 STATEMENTS THAT APPLY

High alignment: You strongly reflect this archetype. These behaviors show up often and impact your leadership presence and team dynamics.

4–7 STATEMENTS THAT APPLY

Moderate alignment: Some tendencies are present for you. You may slip into this archetype when you feel stressed by a specific event or person. With awareness, you can adjust and shift away from this energy.

0–3 STATEMENTS THAT APPLY

Low alignment: This archetype isn't dominant in your leadership style. Still, stay aware of these behaviors creeping in under pressure.

PATTERN RECOGNITION

The Micromanager / Control Freak believes that being a great manager means having as much control over their staff as possible. With all the economic uncertainty and layoffs in recent years, it feels like this management style has really grown. In my experience, micromanagement can come from two different places: (1) managers, or (2) company culture—though the managers themselves don't care for it.

When it comes from management, what does it look like? You check in a lot and need frequent status updates with proof because you don't trust your staff. They have to earn your trust; it isn't given right away. You believe that things will go wrong if you're not there to oversee everything. It isn't enough to provide information about a project and the desired outcome; you like to tell people exactly how to do things, step by step. You'll say, "I just need to make a few edits," and then redo their work because you believe your way is best. You want to be on all their calls, present at every meeting, and cc'd on every email. You like to monitor their calendars and watch the clock when it comes to lunch and breaks. This is how you maintain control over everyone and everything. Micromanagers avoid delegating and empowering their employees to lead, but they end up frustrated because they have so much to do and feel like they can't relax.

MY MICROMANAGER STORY

I once had a manager who pretty much left me alone during most of my time in the role because I'm a self-starter and knew what I was doing. I never received a negative review and was often told how great I was at delivering outcomes, creating opportunities for others, and building partnerships that benefited the organization. My one-on-ones (1:1s) typically consisted of my providing information on what I was doing, asking for feedback before moving forward, and sharing how they could be of assistance. I was viewed as someone who owned my area. There were no questions about how I did things or any proof required of my process because, in the end, I delivered.

When the whole department started going through some leadership challenges, my manager began to change how they led and took a Micromanager approach with me. They became more anxious and started to want more control over things they hadn't been interested in before. My schedule came under scrutiny. They began commenting on the length of my lunch breaks. When I worked remotely, I was told to fill in a chart with excruciating details about what I had worked on each hour of the day. Throughout all the issues in the department, I had still delivered, so the new surveillance and attempts to control felt suspicious and insulting.

Looking back, I see how their fear of another major misstep and loss of control ″impacted how they showed up. When I brought up my concerns about the changes, I was met with deflection: This was coming from senior leadership. That could have been the truth or a lie; either way, it didn't change how I felt as a competent, consistent, low-maintenance employee. The pressure my manager was feeling in their role, and possibly coming from their own manager, was now being directed at me, as it had previously been to some colleagues. I felt like a fresh, new target, and my response wasn't to endure; it was to retreat, start using more of my PTO, and do the bare minimum. Soon after, I resigned, as did several people after me.

WHAT'S REALLY GOING ON

As a Micromanager, you find mistakes unacceptable, so you try to avoid them at all costs. Sometimes you will go to the worst-case scenario when thinking about the fallout from a mistake, so you work overtime to prevent that. This could be something you've always struggled with, or it could be the company's culture. People should be able to mess up, but not every environment uses those instances as opportunities to learn. If you make an error, everyone sees it and you get criticized; you don't want that to happen again. You don't want to be perceived as someone who can't cut it in your role, especially if you have a history of success. In your mind, keeping a close watch on your team isn't harassment; you view it as a necessary part of your job.

In some instances, you are stuck in your old role. You excelled as an individual contributor, and they elevated you to the next level. There were no other options for you. Many companies don't have a path forward for people who excel individually. You deserved and earned an opportunity to move up, and usually moving up at work means getting a staff, even if you're not prepared for that. Being a strong individual contributor and a people manager require different skill sets, and that isn't often made clear to people. So many managers learn on the job, as they go, but there should be formal training and development. Have your employers set you up for success as a leader by making this investment in you? What steps have you taken to advocate for that investment? When this development is missed, many people struggle. When you're struggling, you may look for areas where you can take control and feel powerful, like you used to when your success was about your work, no one else's. Micromanagers can become obsessed with making sure that the people who are doing the work they used to do so well do it the same way they did. This is your area to shine because it's familiar. Unfortunately, in doing so, you neglect growing as a leader and, on top of that, may have no guidance from your leadership. Instead of taking the opportunity to delegate and let others do their job their way, you end up overwhelming yourself. Now you're doing two jobs at once.

Your leadership may put unrealistic expectations on you, or you may have put unrealistic expectations on yourself. The fear of not delivering is kicking your behind, and you don't trust others to get you to where you want and need to be. You may be just as afraid of losing your job as your staff is. We often hear that middle managers will be among the first to go if cuts need to be made, so of course you feel like you have to prove yourself. That energy and pressure are passed down to others, whether intentionally or not. You believe that by hovering over people and keeping a close watch, you can ensure there are no mistakes.

When a team or company is going through a challenging period, managers can find ways to rebuild trust and be more collaborative, but they often don't. During layoffs, for example, a percentage of the staff is removed, leaving the remaining staff to do additional unpaid work, all while under pressure to do well. You know you have fewer people and the same amount of work (or more), and now you decide you want to monitor every move the staff makes and track everything they do. It's a way to control people because things aren't going the way you want and you aren't getting the same results you've gotten in the past when working independently.

As a manager, you have a really great opportunity to develop other people—trust in their ability to be just as great individually as maybe you were! If you weren't a star individual contributor yourself, that's fine too; leading a team could be where you thrive. As an individual contributor, your success was based on your performance. You had control over how you achieved results, unless you were working for a Micromanager yourself. Reflect on how you've been led, and consider whether you felt treated fairly, with some level of autonomy. It's possible that your approach is what was taught to you by your current or previous managers. If you've ever felt frustrated about how you were allowed to approach your work, realize the power you have now to stop the cycle of control. Each person on your team is learning and will make mistakes, which is why having a great leader is a huge plus. Commit to building trust with your staff and viewing them as individuals who aren't you. There is no one-size-fits-all approach to leadership—that's one thing that can make it feel so hard.

WHAT THEY WON'T TELL YOU

- "Even though I'm at a new company now with an amazing culture, I still have PTSD and moments of doubt from my old boss."
- "I worked in social services with victims of violent crimes. . . . We were constantly micromanaged and/or screamed at. . . . Still so hard to understand how we could be treated so badly doing really difficult work."
- "The anxiety, stomach issues, tears is not worth it. The good salary is not worth it. The trauma after going through it is not worth it."
- "A couple years ago I was surviving, thinking I had to stay with a toxic micromanaging supervisor and

no leadership from the top! I left, with mixed feelings. On one hand thinking I failed at surviving, on the other hand thinking F u all, I'm out."

BASED ON A TRUE STORY: MICROMANAGED EMPLOYEE NO. 1

No matter what I do, it's never enough. I've started to feel more like a child than an adult. I know what I'm doing—at least, I used to think that. I'm not sure now. I don't trust myself anymore in this role, and it takes so much longer for me to do things than it did before. I double- and triple-check everything because I know you'll find something wrong. After all my checking, you still find something or come up with some reason to redo it. I actually have gotten worse in this role because I keep finding mistakes, and that didn't used to happen. I used to stretch myself, be more creative, really go for it, but I can't do that now. I don't feel very creative. I do feel you watching me, though. All the time, on my back.

Can I speak? Some of what's going on doesn't make sense, but it's not even worth bringing up because I know you'll do your own thing. I used to be excited about my work; I wanted to be put on these projects, but now I wish you would get someone else to do this stuff. When you know what you put forth is going to be picked apart, it's humiliating. It's embarrassing to get hired to do a job then have someone not trust you to do that work. I was qualified for this role; I have the skills and experience—I just don't know what happened. Well, you don't trust me.

But please believe that I'm giving this one hundred percent and definitely have been putting in the hours to do my best. It's hard to work for someone who doesn't trust me. I see all the issues around here, and I do have ideas on how to fix them, but what's the point? I don't want to meet with you to talk about any of this because I hate meeting with you. You just don't get it. I wish I could work in a different department, or somewhere else. I could start fresh and get back to being the creative, skilled, and confident person I used to be before I started working for you.

BASED ON A TRUE STORY: MICROMANAGED EMPLOYEE NO. 2

I'm getting sick of this. Of you. I know you can tell because I'm short with you. I don't have time for this anymore. Notice how I'm not immediately responding to you anymore? How I can't make it to all of your meetings? I'm not giving you any more opportunities to make me look like a fool in front of everybody.

When you really push me to be at these meetings, be careful, because you'll get what you get. You'll get my sarcasm, you'll get called out, or you'll get nothing. I'm good at sitting in silence, and I love to turn my camera off on Zoom. That way you can't see my eyes rolling. Not that I even care anymore if you do see my facial expressions. You keep poking and pushing me; it feels like you want a reaction. If you want my respect, learn to give it. I've worked hard to get here, and to be honest, you didn't even train me!

The training was some tiring week of watching videos and other nonsense, but I don't even learn that way. You didn't ask me how I like to learn. You threw some one-size-fits-all approach at me, and it wasn't effective. So now you don't trust me. You should have built trust in the beginning, but you didn't, so now this is all on you. You should be glad I figured out how to do this job with no real direction because you were too busy. And now every day you're frantic about things not being exactly to your liking?

I notice you've been taking credit for some of my work; that's why I don't give you ideas anymore. You don't seem qualified to be the manager. I'm documenting everything, every interaction, every time you pick apart my work, because you are the one not to be trusted. You're watching me, and now I'm watching you. I'm going to match your energy because if I have to feel terrible every day at work, so will you. We've all been talking about you. There are real issues here, and you're focused on all the wrong things—it's sad.

HOW TO MAKE THE SHIFT FROM MICROMANAGER TO STRATEGIC DELEGATOR

1. Name your fears and doubts about your ability to succeed. Many of us have one or more fears, and we can't push through them if we don't acknowledge what they are. Where do your fears come from? This doesn't need to be shared with anyone; just take the time to reflect. What is your Micromanager origin story? Who taught you that people can't be trusted?

2. Once you acknowledge your fears, get real about how serious things would be if errors happen or if your manager gets upset with you about a

missed goal. Are these normal experiences in the workplace, or are they career ending? Even if your leadership doesn't give you grace or room to grow, commit to offering that to yourself.

3. Let go of your need for control, and delegate instead! You have a team of one or more people, and they are there to help the company meet its goals, help you become successful as a leader, and meet their own growth and development goals. Choose one project or task to delegate right now. Let them do it. Don't hover. Chill out!
4. Give proper energy to your current role, not any previous one. As an individual contributor, your main focus was delivering personal results. As a manager, your main focus is helping others to perform and grow. How your team performs, works together, and feels lets others know how successful you are as a leader. While you may still have tasks and responsibilities similar to those of your staff (a tough position many managers face), much of your time should be focused on coaching others, reviewing their work, and attending a ridiculous number of meetings.
5. Get to know your staff. Find out, individually, how people learn and like to work. Some of your staff may want more of your involvement, whereas others are fine with you being more hands off. It's never too late, and having these conversations can show your staff you're open to their input and curious about how they prefer to work. If you have

a history of micromanagement, be patient. This won't be easy because they probably don't trust you and will likely be suspicious in the beginning.

6. Dig into the training offered at your company. Some micromanagers share that their employees truly don't do a good job. Some of your current staff may be able to offer insights into what did and didn't work during training—if there was any at all. Give the proper training, time, and attention when someone is new to the role. Provide retraining for existing employees.
7. Think like a coach. Whether you're giving feedback, having a check-in, or having conversations with your team members, act as a coach. Asking open-ended questions will help them think through why they do things a certain way and help you understand and respect it.

    Ask questions like the following:

    - How did you approach this?
    - What felt hardest about this?
    - What support would be useful right now?

    Avoid questions like the following:

    - Why didn't you do it this way?
    - Wouldn't it have been better to . . . ?

    Some questions show curiosity, while others still highlight your desire for some control or suggest that your way would have been best. Give people space to think. They may need help but don't need you to do it for them. Ask them when they want input from you and when they want the freedom to do things their way.

3

The Absentee Manager / Ghost

IS THIS YOU?

- ☐ I don't believe in micromanaging, so I let my staff do their thing.
- ☐ Everyone is an adult. I don't have time to hold people's hands.
- ☐ I was a self-starter; they should be too.
- ☐ The best way for people to learn how to do their jobs is to just do them.
- ☐ I stay out of the way so they can figure it out.
- ☐ My team members can and should coach each other instead of always relying on me.
- ☐ People will come to me if they need help.
- ☐ I have too much work to do and don't have much time for 1:1s.

- ☐ I don't know that much about my team members' goals or challenges.
- ☐ I've been surprised by someone resigning; I didn't see it coming.

8–10 STATEMENTS THAT APPLY

High alignment: You strongly reflect this archetype. These behaviors show up often and impact your leadership presence and team dynamics.

4–7 STATEMENTS THAT APPLY

Moderate alignment: Some tendencies are present for you. You may slip into this archetype when you feel stressed by a specific event or person. With awareness, you can adjust and shift away from this energy.

0–3 STATEMENTS THAT APPLY

Low alignment: This archetype isn't dominant in your leadership style. Still, stay aware of these behaviors creeping in under pressure.

PATTERN RECOGNITION

Some people would love to report to an Absentee Manager / Ghost. When people feel settled in their roles and aren't trying to advance, they don't mind being left alone to do their jobs. This isn't the case for everyone, though. There are employees who would benefit from a different type of leadership, and managers need to be able to adapt to the various needs of their team.

If you're an Absentee Manager, you believe your staff can figure things out because they are competent adults. Sometimes you're just too busy and believe that if someone needs something, they'll ask. "You got this," "Let me know if you need anything," and "Do your thing" are common phrases you say. You don't prioritize your staff's development because you believe development is something people should do for themselves if they want to grow. You really don't want to meet with your staff very often, if at all. If one of them puts a meeting on your calendar, you'll try to reschedule or cancel it. You don't pause to think about your staff's workload, either. You say yes to everything and pass that work right on down to your team.

One of your worst areas is giving feedback because you don't know much about what anyone is doing. You're detached from your staff and don't know their accomplishments. You want your staff to write their reviews so you can sign off on them because, as I said, you don't know what's going on. You know you need to appear in the know, so you power through with a bunch of words and push out some generic review that could apply to anyone. You aren't interested in or knowledgeable about being a mentor or coach, and you might ghost your team during tough times—they will have to figure things out on their own.

MY ABSENTEE-MANAGER STORY

I'm not ashamed to admit I was once an Absentee Manager. I didn't even realize it until about the last week of my role, once my contract ended. This was my first direct management role, and I had to interview and hire staff, something I'd never done before, for the position reporting to me.

I was hired into this role and learned as I went along. My experience up to that point was mainly as an individual contributor. I had worked in the events and hospitality industry and served as the on-site event manager during events, but I had never been anyone's actual boss. I had never done reviews and was never responsible for anyone's day-to-day work or outcomes in a role.

So, when I got my first management role, I hired someone who was fantastic. This person was very bright and just so on it. I thought to myself, I don't really need to do much here; they can just jump right in, and I can do me. Since I'm the kind of person who likes others to be hands off with me, I assumed (incorrectly) that that's how most people want to work. That was my biggest mistake in that role—assuming someone on my staff would enjoy working the same way I do, and on some level, feeling they should work that way. In my head, I was thinking, Why would you really want your boss around, uninvited?

I learned that you have to do three things with all new hires: (1) train them thoroughly, no matter how sharp you think they are, (2) ask them how they like to be managed, and (3) ask how they like to be rewarded. Once they get acclimated, you can collaborate with them on how often they would like to have check-ins. This was a contract role, so near the end of our time together, a group of us were wrapping up, and my employee jokingly made the comment, "Tanya, you never stop into my office to check on me, so you wouldn't even know. Ha ha ha."

Ha ha ha . . . Yeah, they laughed, I laughed, but inside I was like, WHAT? Had I not been aware of or in tune with something because I never really checked in or had any formal sit-down conversations? This wasn't going to be my employee for years, but yeah, I could have made time for them. We could have met weekly to check in, but I mainly talked to them in passing, like a quick "Is everything OK?" as I walked past their office. I also communicated mainly via email.

I knew what they had interest in doing, and I encouraged them to run with it and let me know how I could support them. They never asked me for assistance, and I was OK with that. I figured they didn't need me. A part of me was nervous about being a manager, and I was worried that there would be questions I couldn't answer. Keeping some distance would force them to figure it out without me. Just a mess. After that "joke," I realized that they did want more of my time and attention. I learned a very valuable lesson. I don't want people to think that as their manager, I don't care to talk to them or am too busy or too good to give them proper time and attention. I personally don't need a lot of attention at work, but I'm also further along in my career than others. Much of what someone wants and needs depends on their level of experience, and this person was entry level, so that guidance and mentoring was important. I didn't adapt to the needs of my staff, and I should have.

WHAT'S REALLY GOING ON

There are several types of Absentee Managers: those who are absent because they don't care about being a manager, those who just genuinely don't know how to be a manager because they weren't prepared, and those who are burned out and need to either step down or get their management groove back.

Becoming a manager simply for money, power, or a title isn't unheard of; this is how folks climb that ladder. Personally, I'm not too mad at it because many companies leave you no choice. If they don't offer pathways for individual contributors, people will choose management because we need to move up and get paid. If you want to grow and an opportunity presents itself, why not try it? The thing is, if you're going to be a manager, you need to have some sort of interest in people. Viewing your staff as just a stepping stone to your next, best move is selfish, and it's not easy to hide. I know you're not interested in petty interpersonal conflicts among your staff. I know you don't want to be anyone's coach or therapist. You do have to spend time with people, though; you do have to hear them out and become a problem solver.

Try not to get too offended here, but let's be real, some of you were put into your positions because you were simply the favorite—a good, safe bet employee. They needed you in that role to push their agenda without question or complaint. Others of you just excelled as individual contributors, so you were "rewarded" with a management opportunity. Ultimately, managers like you don't know what you're doing because you weren't prepared, and that's not entirely your fault. There's something so backward about promoting people into management yet offering no development or preparation for the role. People get promoted due to potential, likability, optics—who knows; it just depends on the company. We end up with too many managers who get into these roles while thinking, "I don't know how to do this." It's scary because people look to managers for answers and guidance that you aren't comfortable providing.

It's no shocker that if you never developed coaching or relationship-building skills, you tend to keep some distance from your staff. You can be transactional with your team, wanting to focus solely on the work and not feeling a need to spend that much time with them. Some of my introverted friends could show up as absent without realizing it, depending on their level of introversion. It's easy for introverts to be exhausted from a lot of contact with others, so if you have a big team and a lot of responsibilities, energetically it can be hard to show up for everything and everybody. This will depend heavily on how self-aware you are and how effective you are at managing your time and energy.

Some of the saddest Absentee Managers are those who are burned out. There was a time when you were more present, but you don't have it in you anymore. You could be going through a tough time in your life and unable to give your team what they need. People forget that managers are not only human, but some also have integrity. They may not agree with all the plans and decisions made, but they are often expected to be the face of those plans and decisions, or at the very least, to sell them. If things truly go against their values, they don't want to do that, but the bills must be paid.

Anyone on a payroll can be disengaged, but when you're a manager, there's more at stake. You can't rest and hide unnoticed as easily as others can. You are the person people look to, and you may not want that anymore when you're struggling yourself. You're there physically, but mentally, emotionally, and energetically, you're gone. I've been in that position. I've been overwhelmed by the toxicity within the leadership at a company and had so many days in those roles when I just couldn't do it. I was trying to advocate for people while trying to be the best version of myself, but I was struggling under the same mess that my staff was struggling with, and there was nothing I could do about it. That helpless feeling can cause you to distance yourself from your staff. This is when you start saying things like "We can meet if you want to," and you're really hoping they don't want to. This is when you start putting more responsibility on your staff, like "You all got it; I trust in you to figure it out." We love a trusting manager, but if you're doing this because you don't have the energy to be involved in their work, you don't want to make another decision, and you don't want to manage another project, this isn't about trying to empower anyone. You just don't want to be bothered and want them to do their work while you hide in your office, looking for a new job.

WHAT THEY WON'T TELL YOU

- "I just left a job like this. The manager's negligence was causing all sorts of trickle-down problems for the department."
- "My boss talks a good game but in reality, she's insecure in her role and can't remember anything."
- "Worked for a place for three years and never had a review. I was required to have a three and six months and that was it. Nothing after that."
- "This is my manager. The last two years on my review he literally put under advice for next

year—keep doing what you're doing. Like that was legit my review."

- "I've been in my job for four months and my manager has been of no support to me whatsoever. I've had little to no training so who's fault is it if I make the occasional mistake?"

BASED ON A TRUE STORY: ABSENTEE-MANAGED EMPLOYEE NO. 1

I may as well be self-employed. You don't check on me; you offer no guidance. I really have to figure this all out on my own. Maybe that's how you came up in your career, but it is very uncomfortable for me. I need support. I know you have goals for yourself, and I respect that, but I have goals too and don't quite know how to get to where I want to be. I think I'm doing pretty well, and I try to tell you, but you never seem interested. I have some cool ideas and a way to address the issue we're having with our clients, but there's no one here to go to. You keep postponing our meetings; I think we'll only meet at review time. It would help me to know how I'm doing before then. I keep replaying the past in my head, wondering if I did something to offend you or if you just don't like me for some reason. I'm pulling back with my work because I don't see the point—all these ideas and no one to share them with. You keep giving me more work, but you don't even give me feedback on anything. I don't want any more projects. What am I supposed to be focusing on? Is anyone else struggling here? I think I'm the only one you don't really like.

BASED ON A TRUE STORY: ABSENTEE-MANAGED EMPLOYEE NO. 2

How are you getting paid more than me to be the manager when you aren't managing anything? I could be in a totally different role now and making more money if I worked for someone who understood their job description or just gave a damn. I'm so tired of hearing people say I have to "manage up." You don't know me, you don't know what I'm working on, so you don't advocate for me to get raises—but I'm supposed to do more work? I get that you may not like working here or being a manager, but I don't like that your vibes are rubbing off on me.

Since you started checking out, I started to check out. We all have. This team really has gone downhill. We could use a boost, but you're in your own world. I'm definitely going to be using my PTO to get away from here and look for other jobs. I've told a few folks to beware of joining this team because you're just not present. I hate that I've missed out on reporting to a leader who develops staff and pours into them. When review time comes, you either have nothing to say or find something negative, which is a joke. How can you be gone all the time, yet find something to complain about? I think I'm going to become a manager myself. I know how important it is to develop people instead of forcing them to do that one hundred percent for themselves. Yeah, let me pull back from you and this role and focus on my next steps away from here.

HOW TO MAKE THE SHIFT FROM ABSENTEE MANAGER TO ENGAGED LEADER

1. Acknowledge the type of Absentee Manager you are. Why do you ghost your team? We went over the

different types of Absentee Managers, so identifying which type resonates the most with you is important. Once you do that, start some journaling, or go ahead and talk to yourself out loud so you can get answers. Get to the root of your issue in order to move forward:

- Are you distant from your team because you don't have time for them?
- What is stopping you from making time?
- Do you keep a distance from your team because you don't have the answers to the questions you think they have?
- How can you engage with them with limited knowledge and maintain (or build) their respect for you?
- Do you understand what the role of manager really is?
- How can you gain more understanding and help?
- Are you just over it and don't really want to be a manager anymore?
- What steps will you take to get reinvigorated around leadership or step away from this type of work?

2. Schedule 1:1s with your staff. In the beginning, you may have to meet with people more regularly, but over time you can decrease it based on people's needs. You don't need to spend the same amount of time with everyone.

3. Stop using the excuse that you don't have time, because you will make the time moving forward. These 1:1s don't need to be an hour long! Even fifteen to twenty minutes can be worthwhile if you cut all the small talk and get to business.
4. If you have a large staff and are introverted, time and energy management is key. Identify the time of day when your energy is highest, because that could be the ideal time to meet with people.
5. Acknowledge your absence with your team, and if you're feeling courageous, explain why. It's important that you stay consistent and avoid canceling without rescheduling, and don't cancel very often.
6. Get comfortable saying, "I don't know, but I'll find out or figure it out with you." No one expects you to have all the answers. You'd be surprised how many of your staff would respect you just for being present and honest about what you know—or don't know and will get answers to. One of the great things about management is that you get to grow with your team, and you will learn as much from them as they will from you. Avoiding them actually does more damage to them than being right there with them, willing to learn and mess up. While some may disagree, you don't need to know how to do the jobs of the people on your team. You're there to make sure you meet goals, and you are their coach along the way. They will have answers

that you don't, and they will be smarter and more talented than you in different areas. Wonderful.

7. Commit to learning. For many, like myself, you learn as you go with no real guidance. Your current and previous employers may have dropped the ball, but we don't have time to wallow in that. Pick up some books and read about management and leadership, seek out mentors, find leadership development programs, and advocate for your employer to invest in you. Pick one book (this one counts as a start!), one course, and one training every quarter to grow as a leader.
8. What do people need to feel supported by you? The only way to know is to ask them. Try to be less transactional and more curious about how people are doing. A simple "How are you feeling about your workload?" can do a lot to make people feel like you care. You may not want to hear the answer to this question, but at least acknowledge where they may feel overwhelmed and try to come up with a solution together.
9. On the flip side, you may find that you have staff who want to do more to level up themselves, so figure that out together. Staff like this can take the lead during some meetings or run some training. You should be present, but you're not the only leader in the room. This is how you can shift from reactive vibes of apathy and avoidance to more intentional vibes rooted in compassion and

collaboration. Be mindful not to go too far to the dark side and become a Micromanager!

10. Recognize people. If you're not very present, you're missing opportunities to see the contributions people are making and to call those out. Don't just do this for the obviously visible people; look to your quieter staff as well. Once you start meeting more with people, you'll hear more about what they're doing. Decide how you will recognize people in specific, real ways that they are comfortable with. Some people don't like public recognition; others are OK with it. The key is to never assume—just go ahead and ask what people want.
11. If you're checked out, let's get to the bottom of why. It's normal for people to feel burned out, overwhelmed, or stuck in a role. You're going to have to work to get your energy back because your drop in energy is contagious. Reevaluate what it is that you want and figure out whether you want to stay on the management track or if you're more suited for an individual contributor role. If you want to stay in management, whether within the same company or a different one, you will have to find ways to motivate, encourage, and develop yourself first before you can do that for anyone else.
12. The people who report to you shouldn't have to miss out because you are over it. You chose a path that wasn't the right one for you, or your time is up at the company. As long as you continue to be in a leadership role, you have a responsibility to the

people you lead. I recommend getting in tune with your values and getting back to why management was the route you chose, which we'll address later. Knowing what's ultimately important to you and how you can let that drive you in your work, even if you're not happy with the company, is powerful.

4

The Spotlight Seeker / Credit Stealer

IS THIS YOU?

- ☐ I feel pressure to compete for recognition or visibility.
- ☐ I worry about becoming less relevant or essential over time.
- ☐ I've noticed people are sharing fewer ideas around me.
- ☐ When reporting up, I focus more on outcomes than on who contributed to them.
- ☐ I hesitate to advocate for my staff to get promotions or raises.
- ☐ I assume leadership naturally just comes with more recognition.
- ☐ I'm more comfortable speaking on behalf of my team than having them speak for themselves.

- [ ] I feel uneasy when someone on my team draws a lot of attention for their success.
- [ ] When I'm personally praised for work that was a team effort, I don't rush to correct that.
- [ ] I've shared ideas without clearly crediting their original source.

8–10 STATEMENTS THAT APPLY

High alignment: You strongly reflect this archetype. These behaviors show up often and impact your leadership presence and team dynamics.

4–7 STATEMENTS THAT APPLY

Moderate alignment: Some tendencies are present for you. You may slip into this archetype when you feel stressed by a specific event or person. With awareness, you can adjust and shift away from this energy.

0–3 STATEMENTS THAT APPLY

Low alignment: This archetype isn't dominant in your leadership style. Still, stay aware of these behaviors creeping in under pressure.

PATTERN RECOGNITION

As a Spotlight Seeker / Credit Stealer, you believe you need to shine and are desperate to show your value at all costs. To you, recognition seems to be something in limited supply, so you have to grab as much as you can. You love a "we" or "I" statement, when it should be "they." "We made this happen in a short amount of time." "I have an idea." Do you? It's normal for you to present other people's work as your own. Any opportunity to lift other people up and give them credit publicly is an opportunity you won't take. You make sure your team members don't get much access to leadership or have any real visibility. Everything needs to go through you and be presented by you.

If you look at any job description that says "fast-paced environment," expect Spotlight Seekers to be present. Certain industries are guaranteed to have a lot of credit stealing going on: nonprofits, entertainment, startups, finance, law—all of them! Dealing with clients or with creativity? Spaces where storytelling is important? The spotlight is everything. It's about who is seen, not who is doing the work.

As a Spotlight Seeker, you are so cool, calm, and even charming! The way you speak sometimes, you'll have your staff questioning for a moment where their own ideas originated. The slick way you describe their role—"The team was struggling to push through this and come up with a solution, but I was able to turn it around and ensure we did." The way you insert yourself and inflate your contributions is something. It happens fast, too. You'll move on to the next topic while your staff are still in the meeting trying to figure out if what they saw actually happened.

MY SPOTLIGHT-SEEKER STORY

I once volunteered for a nonprofit while I had a full-time job. I was no longer interested in the type of work I was doing and thought it would be cool to pour into something other than my 9 to 5. I respected the nonprofit and volunteered to assist with one of their new programs.

The following year I was asked to return, and I was excited because I had some ideas on how to expand and improve the program. A new manager had been hired, and I shared my ideas with them. My hope was that my ideas would be implemented, but I was also just a volunteer and figured they had their own plans. I too had plans and was going to leverage my volunteer experience to secure a role elsewhere doing similar work.

The new manager never said anything to me about implementing my ideas or expressed any agreement, but over time I noticed that more of what I recommended had become part of the program. My ideas were rolled out as updates and expansion led by the new manager. They never mentioned me or my contributions. At the time, I was disturbed by this, but I questioned myself. Was it OK for them to do that and not credit me because I was just a volunteer?

Over time, I became more and more disgusted because people liked the updates, and the manager took the credit, happily. This happens all the time in the workplace. For me as a volunteer, and of course not getting paid, watching someone else make money off my ideas and framework felt violating. I spent more time explaining to myself that this person was new and wanted to make a good first impression in their role than advocating for myself—something that happens when people experience shock, confusion, and disgust in their full-time jobs when their managers do the same thing.

As a Spotlight Seeker, you are so charismatic and such a great talker that you easily get into a role and can lean on, or straight up use, others around you to grow and get accolades. It's frustrating for others to watch, but you have learned how to play the game. You know better than anyone that optics mean more than talent in many companies, and you use likability to your advantage.

WHAT'S REALLY GOING ON

As a Spotlight Seeker, you know what you are doing is wrong, but you tell yourself there's no other way to show your value at work, especially if talent isn't your strong suit. Being viewed as valuable is everything to you, and there's a part of you that may feel it's OK, as the manager, to take the credit. I wonder how many of you have experienced being overlooked or undervalued and vowed never to let that happen again. You may not have the level of skill or knowledge for your particular role, but you need to make it work because the goal is to just keep moving up. You're willing to do some things that others may not do to get to where you're going. For you, the workplace is a competitive space, so in your mind, it makes sense that everybody's got to do what they've got to do.

A big fear here is irrelevance, or being outshone. Scarcity thinking can run rampant within you. If you're working in environments where the promotions are limited or just hard to get, and add to that your need for validation, there's no time to be naming names. You question what would happen if you didn't present the work as yours. What happens if your staff rises above you and is viewed as more valuable? As the manager, you might even have convinced yourself that if you hadn't been there to lead them in some way, they wouldn't have been able to come up with these ideas and produce this work.

In other scenarios, deep down, you question your qualifications for the role. Maybe you don't think you're as smart as others, and you don't want anybody to find out, so you take from your staff and present everything as if it were yours alone. You may actually bring value, but there's no chance to see it.

Maybe you had to compete for attention or praise in your youth, so you are still out here competing with your own staff. Maybe you worked for some poor leaders early in your career, and they showed you how it's really about who is the most visible, not who's the most talented, so you've decided not to focus on being talented yourself. You may be missing out on opportunities to show what you've got because you continue to grab from others.

There are people on your team who are so talented and should be elevated off your team into something else, but you won't let them go. If you do, you're going to lose out on what they've been feeding you, or what you've just been taking from them. Some people have their identity wrapped up in what they produce, and you struggle with this more than most. The only way you feel worthy is when others validate you. Imagine how this impacts your team, and consider how long it will be before they stop giving their all.

WHAT THEY WON'T TELL YOU

- "Going through this now and I feel so frustrated. The idea that was taken was one that definitely would have aided my visibility. Not sure how to address it."
- "I had a boss like this and every time I did some work they would take credit and prevent me from sharing it with the entire team."
- "Let the people on your team shine."

- "I used to work so hard and get my ideas stolen by people that felt I was a threat to them for some reason. Instead of collaborating and doing great things, they tried to make me play small."
- "I see it every day, people start taking my work and making it seem they came up with the ideas. That's why I play dumb and shut my mouth now."

BASED ON A TRUE STORY: SPOTLIGHT SEEKER–MANAGED EMPLOYEE NO. 1

I'm speechless. I can't believe my work is being presented as theirs when I did all of this. I feel violated. Why would they do this? I always felt like we got along, so this is throwing me. I guess because they are my manager this is normal? I'm not really sure, and it doesn't feel right. I want to say something, but I don't want to make our relationship weird or face any backlash. I like my job and don't want to disrupt this. It's just that I work hard and wouldn't mind being recognized. They are more senior and more experienced, so maybe I need them to be the face of this work. I wonder if they will help me move up based on what I've done. It does seem like they keep getting the kudos, though, and may be moving up without me. Now that this has happened repeatedly, I'm just going to pull back. I don't want to keep doing all this work when it's not acknowledged. It's also wild that none of my coworkers said anything on my behalf—they know what I've done. Everyone just sits there. I guess they figure since I didn't say anything on my own behalf the first time, they aren't going to speak up for me. I don't trust anyone here anymore; I guess I don't have friends at work.

BASED ON A TRUE STORY: SPOTLIGHT SEEKER-MANAGED EMPLOYEE NO. 2

The more I see this, the angrier I get. We're all adults, and we're stealing at work? This goes beyond eating someone's food from the refrigerator (although that's messed up too); you are taking credit for something that has real value. You're using me to get ahead and clearly have no plans to bring me up with you. You have no shame. You think that you're entitled to my ideas and work simply because you're my boss. Who told you this? I'm starting to move in a different way now. Let me starve you of ideas and information so everyone can see what you're made of. Not only am I not going to help you anymore, but I'm not helping anyone here. I see how people get ahead in this company—by pretending to be talented, not by actually being talented. I used to think it was in poor taste to go above people, but I'll make sure to let it be known that I'm the one responsible for what has been put out. I guess I'll have to cc folks so they know I'm part of the team too. Your manager would want to know, and I have nothing to lose at this point. I'll put together a portfolio of what I've done that will be useful in my job search.

HOW TO MAKE THE SHIFT FROM CREDIT STEALER TO CREDIT GIVER

1. Identify your fear(s). You may have a fear of becoming irrelevant, being overshadowed, being

replaced, being exposed, and so on. These thoughts and feelings that can be shifted.

2. Take note of any and all moments when you feel discomfort because someone on your team is praised. What do you feel, and why? Jealousy is a normal feeling; just acknowledge it and push through. How do you push through that? Smile and praise people anyway, even when it pains you. You can work through those feelings alone, however it is comfortable for you (writing, reflection), or you can work with a professional to get to the bottom of them. It's not your staff's responsibility to carry the weight of your feelings of inadequacy—or whatever else you are dealing with. Work on it privately, but publicly champion everyone on your team!
3. Consider that your team winning would actually highlight how strong a leader you are. You can pour into each and every one of your team members, showcase them, advocate for them, and be known as the leader who creates other leaders. A lot of people give credit to managers who support, motivate, inspire, and push them to be great. This is a huge part of your job! If you have a need to be in the spotlight, go back to being an individual contributor. Think about where this need for the spotlight and validation comes from. It's possible to shift your mindset about what makes you valuable.
4. Build empathy. Sometimes it's simply a matter of trying to put ourselves in someone else's shoes. How would you feel if someone took credit for

something you'd done? If this has happened to you, how did it make you feel? Consider that it hits your team members very hard even if they smile and tell you otherwise. People don't have to tell you that something is wrong for you to imagine that it is. Assume people aren't OK with the theft, and adjust your behavior accordingly.

5. Understand what a scarcity mindset is. This is when people believe there is a limited supply of something—in this case, a limited amount of recognition, value, visibility, promotions, and more. Even if your company is very small, there is still room for both you and your staff to be great at the same time. There are no limits to what you can do or where you can go. If the thinking is that if someone else wins, you'll lose, you will never feel at peace! Consider adopting an abundance mindset instead—the belief that there's enough for everyone. Everyone can win, and some people don't even believe there are winners and losers in any situation.
6. Make a list of the past wins and great things that have come from your team and department. If there are any people who were not properly credited for their work or ideas, correct that now. This is something that sounds and would feel good, but I know some of you won't do it. Others of you have it in you to do so, and this could be one of the most amazing things you do in your career. Moving forward, name the people who were involved. Stop saying "I" or "we" if it's not accurate. Start taking

notes and giving out specific praise to individuals on your team who do things worth shouting out. The next time someone on your team creates something or has a great idea, let them present it and take ownership of it. This makes both of you look good! Recognition can become a part of your team culture, and any new members of your team should be encouraged to take the same approach to recognition.

7. Comparison can be a big problem. Get clear on your strengths, both as an individual contributor and as a manager. Where do you shine on your own? What are some instances in your career when you have truly been a difference maker or built something that was celebrated? Now that you're the manager, start rethinking how you can continue to be a difference maker while allowing other people to shine.

5

The Gatekeeper / Blocker

IS THIS YOU?

- ☐ I'm overwhelmed and unsupported, so it's hard to show up and support others.
- ☐ I believe that if the workhorses of my team move up, I'll be the one stuck with the extra work.
- ☐ It bothers me a bit when people on my staff get recognized or praised by senior leaders.
- ☐ I tend to develop people I personally relate to versus those with the most potential.
- ☐ I don't have a clear successor on my team, but I haven't really helped build one either.
- ☐ Sometimes I ignore the career goals that my staff express to me.
- ☐ I tell people they're "not ready" without offering any insights or support to get them ready.

- ☐ I avoid helping my staff gain exposure to leadership or putting them on high-visibility projects.
- ☐ I don't nominate my high-performing staff for promotions or other opportunities.
- ☐ I've discouraged someone from pursuing an opportunity because losing them would create a problem for me or the team.

8–10 STATEMENTS THAT APPLY

High alignment: You strongly reflect this archetype. These behaviors show up often and impact your leadership presence and team dynamics.

4–7 STATEMENTS THAT APPLY

Moderate alignment: Some tendencies are present for you. You may slip into this archetype when you feel stressed by a specific event or person. With awareness, you can adjust and shift away from this energy.

0–3 STATEMENTS THAT APPLY

Low alignment: This archetype isn't dominant in your leadership style. Still, stay aware of these behaviors creeping in under pressure.

PATTERN RECOGNITION

Like Absentee Managers, Gatekeepers / Blockers aren't very engaged or supportive. Absentee Managers aren't usually intentional about that, though. As a Gatekeeper, you are doing it on purpose. You actively work to keep your employees right where you want them—usually in positions that aren't beneficial or fair to them but keep you quite comfy. You know people would benefit from more opportunity or visibility, but you block those efforts. It's obvious when a member of your staff is ambitious and wants to earn more and take on more, but you always ignore their calls for help because you want to control how someone rises or if they rise at all.

As a Gatekeeper, you believe that people aren't ready until you say they're ready, which likely will never happen. The carrot will be dangled, though. People reporting to you will believe they are doing the right work the right way. They think their time is coming, but it never does. You intentionally don't teach or train people on certain aspects of their jobs because you don't want them to replace you. You may carry the same attitudes as some of our elders, who think that because they had to struggle and fight, everyone has to. To you, this is all part of the game at work. You are quick to pump the brakes on any promotion talk that comes up from ambitious staff, especially those you are threatened by. "Just keep doing what you're doing" and "You need more time; you're not ready yet" are common phrases from you. You'll never actually tell people what "ready" means.

No high-visibility projects will go to anyone who isn't one of your favorites. Your favorites are always mentioned, always picked; it becomes expected. If someone who isn't a favorite tries to get in on the action, you find ways to block them. You block mentoring, projects, and opportunities to connect with your leadership. You would never want to assist those on your staff in surpassing you, as you are typically threatened by ambitious people on your team for various reasons. For people on your team who you know are talented yet not ambitious, you are sure to avoid encouraging them to seek advancement. You know who the talent is, and you fear that if they leave the position you want them in, it could expose how much they truly contributed to your team's success—possibly more than you did.

MY GATEKEEPER STORY

I once was part of a management team at an organization where a new position was created. There was someone on the staff who was perfect for that role, and it would have been the next step up for them. They had shown their loyalty, they were consistent, and they had the leadership qualities that would make them a great fit. I was on a different part of the team and wasn't going to be directly impacted by whatever decision was made. I knew all parties involved, and as this was being openly discussed, I was like, "Yes, that would be a great opportunity for them; they'll be so excited." Another colleague agreed and wanted this employee to make the move. Our leader at the time had other plans and hesitated. They said, "If they get promoted into that role, then who's going to do their old job? That position is going to be hard to fill."

My immediate internal reaction was "That's your problem, not theirs!" I was really disgusted and appalled that someone would intentionally hold another deserving person back from moving up and making more money because they didn't have the desire or confidence in their ability to fill that role. I put my two cents in, not sure if my opinion mattered, but I believe we should advocate for others, as we would want them to do for us. In the end, the person got their well-earned promotion. Thankfully, that leader listened to feedback from us as a staff and did the right thing!

Making errors is just part of the job as a manager, but some errors can have a huge effect on an entire department. People may not speak up in the moment, and they may not comment after the fact, but this type of self-centered leadership doesn't go unnoticed. If people see talented and deserving individuals getting overlooked, it can kill morale and also create a team of "bare minimum" employees that folks love to complain about.

WHAT'S REALLY GOING ON

As a Gatekeeper, you may have been in some rough situations in your career. I wonder just how often you were overlooked, disrespected, and unsupported. You might feel like something is owed to you and take it out on your staff without realizing it. Sometimes you're burned out and overwhelmed, so you don't want to add a single piece of extra work to your load. Extra work to you looks like developing people, having 1:1s, hiring, interviewing, and training. Much of the typical work of a manager. If you have a good thing going, you don't want to disrupt that. There can be some selfishness here, along with a desire to see your staff members overwork and put in an obscene amount of time to advance. You may be so stuck on the struggle parts of your own story that you can't bear to watch someone skip that step. You look back on your career and remember the help you didn't have, the opportunities you had to fight for, and now you're in a position of power. Instead of using that power to help people have a different experience, you are unfortunately doing to them what was done to you.

As a Gatekeeper, you have spent so much time in environments where everything was political that you learned you had to play the game to get ahead. As a result, you believe this is normal and acceptable. You had to fight; now others have to pay their dues too. Are you taking a past frustration out on people who aren't responsible for what you endured? Sometimes a scarcity mindset is present, and you believe there isn't room for everyone, so you do everything you can to make sure your spot stays secure. Ambitious staff might annoy you. You lead yourself to believe that employees should be loyal to you and prioritize their relationship with you versus focusing on their own individual growth.

The fears here are of being replaced, being exposed as having limitations, and being irrelevant. You also may have a fear of losing power. Like other problematic managers, you may carry old wounds from being passed over or unsupported, so you in turn do the same to others, sometimes without realizing it. Sometimes you convince yourself that the harmful things you do to others are for their own good. You can really twist things and present them as though you are simply protecting people from failure, or that people will thank you later when they look back and see why you did what you did. Being in charge and in control is important to you, and you will act as though you are doing what's best for everyone when you are actually selfishly doing things for your own benefit and protection.

WHAT THEY WON'T TELL YOU

- "That's the problem with being a good employee, or the 'workhorse.' Managers don't want to lose that employee, so they block them, or never consider them for promotions. I've been the workhorse."
- "Too many exceptional employees leave because of awful managers."
- "I give my 110 percent, yet people who give half get promoted!"
- "I kept working one hundred hours extra for companies and never got appreciated; they just gave me more work. Then when I got burned out and tired of it, they said I wasn't performing my job duties."
- "I've had more opportunities from doing my bare minimum than when I was going above and beyond. My hard work was making others look bad and I was being punished for it."
- "When it's an obvious diss, it really kills the morale of everyone in the department. And more than just that one overlooked person will leave. It also makes me and others lose respect for leadership. That's a huge thing they will never get back."
- "It baffles the mind because nine times out of ten, there is absolutely no chance of you taking that person's job. If I know things, that person should be glad that I can help make their team look good."
- "You can't just do your eight and leave in peace because then you are considered an outsider. You

can't volunteer too much because that makes you an ass-kisser or trying to take another's position. Damned if you do, damned if you don't."

BASED ON A TRUE STORY: GATEKEEPER-MANAGED EMPLOYEE NO. 1

This truly is a dead-end job. I've done everything I'm supposed to do and more, but it has gotten me nowhere here. I thought I was putting forth great work, but maybe not? There just always seems to be a reason I'm not getting a promotion or a raise. I'm seeing people around me who haven't done half of what I've done move up, and I don't get it. I've asked what I should do, and even after doing those things, I get told there's now something else I need to do. It seems like they are looking for perfection from me but no one else. The goalposts keep moving, and it's impossible for me to keep up. I don't know if I chose the right job here or even the right career. I've been thinking of going back to school or getting another certification—maybe then I can't be denied. It's not a guarantee, though. It's actually embarrassing. Everyone can see my work, and people are always telling me how great I am, but my manager seems to downplay it. I'm ambitious but exhausted. I could go work somewhere else, but a job search is going to take so much out of me. The so-called quiet quitters are onto something. My desire to take on another project, do anything extra, is now gone. What's weird is I keep getting overlooked for growth, but they keep giving me more to do.

BASED ON A TRUE STORY: GATEKEEPER-MANAGED EMPLOYEE NO. 2

Now they have me training staff! I'm good enough to train people and share my knowledge, but not good enough to move up? These people are getting promoted over me—I'm basically training my next boss! It's getting too disrespectful now. They want loyalty from me but give me nothing in return. It's feeling intentional. I knew my boss was insecure. So threatened by me; it's sad. These folks getting opportunities are not better than me. I'm no longer accepting vague answers to my questions about what's next for me, and I have proof of everything I've done. None of this can be denied. I've already started talking to other people here so they know what this manager is all about. They are shocked when I tell them how I've been played. I'm looking elsewhere for work, and people will see how messed up things are when I'm not here to do so much.

HOW TO MAKE THE SHIFT FROM GATEKEEPER TO DOOR OPENER

1. Put yourself in someone else's shoes. Have you ever felt like you were being held back? How did it make you feel? Here's your opportunity to break the cycle and ensure other people have a different experience as they try to grow in their careers.
2. Develop a legacy-minded leadership style. When people who report to you shine and succeed, that reflects well on you. It shows that you are a mentor,

a coach, an inspirational person who creates environments where people can thrive and do their best work. That would prove you are an impactful leader who gets results. Think about the challenges you've had in your career and ask yourself, is it truly necessary for someone else to go through the same things?

3. Sponsor people and don't do it half-assed. You may be a mentor to one or many, but there's a lot of power in advocating for people when they aren't around. Mentoring people, particularly at work, isn't the end of how you support people. Push past private mentoring and publicly present people's names and strengths. Recommend people who lead differently from you, not just your typical favored type. Do this with no thought of how they may outshine or move ahead of you. You are running your own race.
4. Embrace the reality that you are meant to be pushed into something bigger and better for yourself. If you believe someone is a threat to you or is potentially going to push you out of your role, then maybe it's time for you to go. Accept that and see the opportunity being presented. Reflect on why you're clinging to a position you can move on from. What has caused you to limit yourself to the role you're in, the company you work for?
5. Deliver specific feedback that people can do something with. Sometimes Gatekeepers nitpick or try to humble their staff, especially their high performers.

That is fear, jealousy, and insecurity talking. When people share their great ideas, encourage them. When you find yourself feeling small because someone else is praised, push through. The moment you look for an issue with someone who is clearly winning and thriving is the moment you let those reactive vibes take over. Let people know the truth about what they can do to make it to the next level or wherever they would like to go.

6. When people tell you how they want to grow and the type of work they'd like to do, direct and support that. You don't get to decide people's futures, and everyone's future isn't tied to you. When you try to control other people's paths, you think you are securing your spot, but you're actually limiting yourself in the process.
7. Stop moving the goalposts. Commit right now to developing clear paths for staff. What does it look like to advance on your team? In your organization? If this is beyond your level of management, take it to higher levels. This should exist within the organization. When it's not clear what people can do to move to the next level, you lose trust and motivation among the staff. People will pull back, and your best employees will leave. You may think that's OK, but your job may be on the line if this happens.

6

The Burnout Creator / Martyr

IS THIS YOU?

- ☐ I'm the first one to arrive and the last to leave. I take pride in that.
- ☐ If I'm not available for people, I feel guilty.
- ☐ It's faster for me to just do things myself; that's why I don't delegate.
- ☐ I don't take much time off or many breaks for myself.
- ☐ The number of hours people put in means more to me than outcomes.
- ☐ I resent people for not working as hard as I do.
- ☐ People who leave right at the end of their workday aren't really trying to get ahead.

- ☐ It rubs me the wrong way when my staff sets boundaries.
- ☐ I've told people to "push through" when they ask for support.
- ☐ I question how dedicated someone can be to their work when they have a child.

8–10 STATEMENTS THAT APPLY

High alignment: You strongly reflect this archetype. These behaviors show up often and impact your leadership presence and team dynamics.

4–7 STATEMENTS THAT APPLY

Moderate alignment: Some tendencies are present for you. You may slip into this archetype when you feel stressed by a specific event or person. With awareness, you can adjust and shift away from this energy.

0–3 STATEMENTS THAT APPLY

Low alignment: This archetype isn't dominant in your leadership style. Still, stay aware of these behaviors creeping in under pressure.

PATTERN RECOGNITION

As a Burnout Creator / Martyr, you resent anyone who has a life away from work because you don't. If you do have a life away from work, you are willing to push it aside for a job or, for some reason, are trying to avoid it. You may be able to afford help with your kids and household responsibilities or simply rely on a partner to manage that. Maybe you don't have much of a family or friends and pour your all into work. Your identity is very aligned with what you do. If someone asks you about yourself, you will likely lead with your job title or company name. If this is the way you feel about work, that's a fine personal choice. It becomes a problem for your staff when there's an expectation for them to mirror your behavior. According to the Burnout Creator, rest is for the weak. You would hate to be viewed as weak and put a lot of pressure on yourself to do it all. To you, the sacrifice is part of the work and part of what a good leader does.

Your favorite employees are those who view work and work/life balance in the same way you do. You believe that you should always stay late, you don't need to take lunch breaks away from your desk, and of course, you should come in on your off days if that's what would be best for the company. Anyone who has a different approach to work—perhaps believing that a job is just a job—or someone with boundaries is viewed as less committed and not worthy of moving up. Beyond your belief about what the company needs, you will tell anyone who will listen that you just have an amazing work ethic. You do this for yourself because you have high standards when it comes to your work. Maybe you were raised that way or mentored by someone who told you this is how you do work. You don't pretend to be busy; you are busy because you don't delegate and will look for things to do. In your mind, no one is as dedicated as you are or may do things as well, so it's best for you to do them yourself.

MY BURNOUT-CREATOR STORY

During my job search, I remember a panel of interviewers commenting on and laughing about how much time they spent at work. They started debating who spent the least amount of time with their family. I must have made a facial expression because one said, "That's just typical for this industry." I knew I wasn't a match and was OK with finding out later that I wouldn't be moving forward in the process. These Burnout Creators will always remind you of how busy they are and how they haven't taken a vacation in sooooooooo long. Again, not a problem for me, except they want others to do what they do. They don't want you to take time off and will resent you for having boundaries because they don't have any. Even if they claim to be OK with people taking time off and not being available on off days, they make it difficult for people to do so. Managers shouldn't just talk about being OK with balance; they should model that behavior so others are comfortable joining in.

Another time, I remember a manager rolling their eyes as they commented on one of my colleagues taking "another vacation," as if this person always used PTO. They actually didn't; they simply saved it for a big trip at the end of the year. I didn't see this as being a big deal because there was always advanced notice, and we are free to use our PTO as we wish—it's part of our compensation package.

Side note: Managers aren't entitled to know how their staff uses their PTO. Whether you're in Fiji or lounging on your couch at home, all they need to know is you won't be at work.

Anyway, I wasn't fully surprised by the snarky comment because this particular manager was very attached to their role and liked to be the last to leave. I always wondered why they couldn't just let things wait until the next day. In the beginning, I thought they were very dedicated to their work, and I thought to myself, "Oh, maybe I should strive for that sometimes." Those thoughts were short-lived because, over time, it seemed like they were annoyed. Sometimes they expressed frustration about not being able to relax and having to do things that no one else could do. I saw no one getting in the way of their relaxation, and people were willing to do more, but they had a hard time letting go of certain tasks. If this is a person's chosen work style, I don't care—until they start to judge or withhold opportunities from those who work in a different way.

WHAT'S REALLY GOING ON

As a Burnout Creator, you just seem committed to and comfortable in the struggle. For some of you, you believe you can't truly be excellent without being exhausted. In your mind, lazy people are the ones who rest. You like looking at your calendar and seeing how booked and busy you are, because to you, busy people are important people. Maybe this is how you were raised or what you've been told by a mentor or someone you idolize. If you're not always putting in the maximum effort, that's a hit to your self-esteem. Your impact matters most, but that's not what you believe, and maybe you've been rewarded for being the most visible, get to work early, leave late, no days off type of employee. You may not like seeing how busy you are, but it's all part of your story. You just have so much to do, no one else can do it, no one supports you, and so on. You believe you are the one who truly gets what it takes to be productive or successful.

Honestly, when you stay so busy like this, you are avoiding reality. The reality of how you really feel. If you slow down, you may have to sit with how tired you actually are and how unappreciated you feel. You've set a certain standard for yourself and possibly others, but you think that once you change, people may look at you in a different way and no longer need you.

Big fears here include being dispensable and having others prove that they don't have to burn out to get results. So much of what you do is tied to that belief, that those who put in the most hours and are the most committed to the job are the ones who do the best. Who told you that? When have you ever had boundaries yourself and been punished for it? An experience or multiple experiences like that, whether work related or not, could cause you to remove boundaries, and then when you become a manager, you resent people who have the audacity to set them.

WHAT THEY WON'T TELL YOU

- "Our expectations for teachers, nurses and other helping professionals are inhumane to be quite honest. Burnout is no joke, it's killing people and making them chronically ill, and we just wash, rinse and repeat. Smh."
- "I internalized the sacrifice and hustle culture of the nonprofit industrial complex so deep, I needed to hit rock bottom to remember who I was and what I'm worth."

- "I wasted eighteen years of my life to resign totally exhausted both mentally and physically."
- "These past years I have experienced many episodes of anxiety, because I felt extremely overwhelmed by all the work that was thrown at me."
- "I realized that management is stressed and they take it out on the staff and then when we respond we get in trouble."
- "The way they have dragged down my esteem is scary for me. Honestly, I just need to leave."
- "Until we got a new part time manager, I used to go into the gym and swim at least four times a week. Now I don't have the energy because of the ridiculous work overload added, and I'm so emotionally exhausted as well. My days off are even occupied by her in my mind."

BASED ON A TRUE STORY: BURNOUT CREATOR-MANAGED EMPLOYEE NO. 1

I can't keep up. I know I'm a hard worker, but this is too much. It's like they forget I'm a person, not a machine, and that I have a whole life away from this job. It seems like the people who are favored and get the most opportunity here are the ones who don't have any boundaries. They make me feel like there's something wrong with me because I'm ready to go when it's time for me to go. I need breaks from here; I'm eating my lunch in my car just for a change of scenery. I'm always looking at jobs online, but I don't apply for anything.

This is the norm in this country—I doubt I would do well anywhere else since every place is basically the same. At least I know what to expect with this manager; I don't even have the energy to figure out someone new.

BASED ON A TRUE STORY: BURNOUT CREATOR-MANAGED EMPLOYEE NO. 2

I'm not coming in early, and I'm not staying late anymore. I don't have to do that to do well because I know how to prioritize my tasks and stay focused. My work is important to me, but I shouldn't have to sacrifice all my relationships and hobbies for this place. They throw way too much at me at the last minute, and it's just so disrespectful of my time and energy. They seem happy to burn themselves out; they wear their overwork like a badge of honor. I've said no thank you to the last few projects here. I don't care if they look at me differently. I'm not like them—that is a fact. They just want carbon copies of themselves, when I'm my own person. This job doesn't define me. I do want to excel at work, but I don't have to be here at all hours to do so. I give my best while I'm supposed to be here and manage my time well, so I do what's most important first, and whatever can wait till tomorrow can wait. You should try that! I've seen how people are treated here when they sacrifice everything for this job, and it doesn't inspire me to do more.

HOW TO MAKE THE SHIFT FROM BURNOUT CREATOR TO BOUNDARY MODELER

1. Redefine hard work. How do you determine when people are performing well? Look at who your

favorites are, who you respect the most. Are they people who put in overtime or stay late consistently? Think about why you believe the hustle is more respected than creativity in someone's process, resourcefulness, and recovery time. Who gets promoted? Burnout Creators promote and praise staff who mirror their unhealthy leadership style. So, you are more likely to praise and promote people who never seem to rest, like you. Start from scratch and get to a definition of success that doesn't include people suffering and not having a life away from work—including you! Think about the people you may have overlooked and shift to a focus on leadership traits as a major factor in who gets rewarded, like how people manage their energy and boundaries; how they delegate; and how they mentor, train, and coach others.

2. Take the lead on rest. You know you get tired. Even if you think you give off the vibe that people can rest and don't have to mirror you, that's not going to happen. People won't rest until they see you do it, so do it! Leave right at the end of your workday. Even if you do it for only a couple of weeks as part of your own experiment, just try it. When your staff sees you leave, they'll feel more comfortable leaving on time too. Set realistic standards not just for your staff, but for yourself. If you have a history of announcing how you worked so many hours last week, were at the office all night working on a project, or came in on an off day, start making new announcements. Try, "I left right at five every

day last week, and it felt good to be so productive during the day that I could. Whatever I didn't finish, I just set aside for the next day. Let's all normalize that."

3. Track your days and how you distribute your energy. Take one week and track how you felt at the end of the day, when you took a break, when you ate something! Then study what you did that day and at what times. You can create three columns: "What I did," "When I did them," and "How I felt." Some things drain us, some energize us, and others are just neutral tasks we can't do anything about; they are just a necessary part of the job—like doing certain reports. Look for patterns and determine what is worth keeping, letting go of, changing, and so on. You can do this with your team also!
4. Pause when your moments of judgment pop up. When an employee tells you about upcoming vacation plans, or when someone makes it a point to regularly leave at the end of their workday, think before you judge. If you feel it's a problem, why? If this employee delivers well in their area and has met their goals, what is truly bothering you? You may find that you often project your habits and values onto others.
5. Build a succession plan. The first step is to create a list of all the things you believe only you can do. Look at your team and, based on what you already know about them and what you'll learn about their interests during 1:1s, start determining who will be

trained on what. You're not going to start randomly dumping extra work onto people; you'll strategically align tasks with their interests where possible. Keep a document that shows what people are working on so they aren't overwhelmed. Start creating opportunities for people to share knowledge so this whole process is collaborative, including shadowing opportunities. Fight for people to receive professional development funds to build skills and grow.

6. Think like a coach! Ask open-ended questions to gain more understanding of why people work the way they do, especially if it's different from your way. Be curious about how they are able to meet goals without burning out—if you actually have anyone on your team who isn't burned out like you. Coaches know they can't control the outcome, and that's a relief. View yourself more as a facilitator; you can facilitate the process of empowering people to work in a healthy way that honors their boundaries, instead of trying to force them to mimic your unhealthy work style.
7. Consider the benefits of a rested team. Instead of thinking that the best workers are those who don't take breaks or vacation time and just push through for what's best for the team or company, try a different view. Rested workers are more creative, focused, and strategic.

7

The Culture Enforcer / Mold Maker

IS THIS YOU?

- ☐ A true leader shapes people to fit the company mold.
- ☐ I go with my gut when it comes to promotions; some people just feel right to me.
- ☐ I tend to reward people who mirror my energy, tone, and style of work.
- ☐ It's a challenge at times to connect with or coach people who are different from me.
- ☐ My feedback is more focused on presence, polish, and vibes versus outcomes.
- ☐ I tend to promote people who are more extroverted and warm.
- ☐ I've mentioned that people aren't ready but haven't given clear reasons why.

- [ ] I worry that people who don't fit my ideal model of leadership will make me look bad if they are promoted.
- [ ] It makes me uncomfortable when someone, especially a woman, is direct or doesn't soften their language.
- [ ] I feel more comfortable when everyone gets along, even if that means some may feel they can't express different opinions.

8–10 STATEMENTS THAT APPLY

High alignment: You strongly reflect this archetype. These behaviors show up often and impact your leadership presence and team dynamics.

4–7 STATEMENTS THAT APPLY

Moderate alignment: Some tendencies are present for you. You may slip into this archetype when you feel stressed by a specific event or person. With awareness, you can adjust and shift away from this energy.

0–3 STATEMENTS THAT APPLY

Low alignment: This archetype isn't dominant in your leadership style. Still, stay aware of these behaviors creeping in under pressure.

PATTERN RECOGNITION

As a Culture Enforcer, you aren't always loud about what you believe; you are more subtle. You quietly come to the conclusion that a leader fits into a very specific box. You have in your mind the ideal look, vibe, mannerisms, tone, and so on that a leader must have to be acceptable and "ready." You often use the phrase "cultural fit" and are focused more on optics than anything else. As a manager, you avoid people who aren't open to conforming, no matter how well they perform. When review time comes, some of your staff will get feedback about their personality, instead of their performance. For example, commenting on someone's facial expressions in meetings. Anyone who doesn't fit your mold of professionalism is slowly but surely excluded. You push people to be palatable, safe bets who align with whatever the dominant culture is in the company. You promote people you like, not the most qualified. This can be a huge issue for assertive women, especially assertive Black women, introverts, neurodivergent folks, and anyone from a historically marginalized group.

Your staff who refuse to conform may be labeled difficult, not a good fit, or not having leadership potential. There's an "us" versus "them" vibe here, where you are an outsider if you don't act the same as everyone else, or at least those in power. These managers will say things like "That's not how we do things here," "You're being a little too direct," or "Be careful how you're coming across." If the environments these Culture Enforcers create don't feel like full-blown cults, they definitely create cliques within their team or company and deal heavily in favoritism. If people value authenticity, they will struggle in these environments with these managers, because everything they do will be labeled as "not a good look."

MY CULTURE-ENFORCER STORY

A colleague of mine was interviewing for a role they were very much qualified for. They had been with the company for years and had actually been doing much of the work already, but they were behind the scenes, in a sense, and not the face of the operation. They had the ideas, the passion, and the credentials. I wondered why they had been in a secondary role for so long when they were actually the driving force behind a lot of what was being produced. I was part of their hiring process, and compared to other candidates, they were my top choice for all the reasons I mentioned. A senior leader said something that I will never forget, especially because it was said out loud: "Their presentation was good, but they don't quite have the polish." It wasn't about their actual presentation; it was about them. I understood what the senior leader meant, and I just hated that not only was it said out loud but so many of us cling to these strict ideals of who a leader can be. I felt some shame within myself because, even if just for a brief moment, I understood what they meant, knew it was wrong, and didn't speak up loudly enough against it. I voiced my view that they were the right person, but I wish I had had the courage to more directly call out the bias behind that senior leader's statement.

Many of us have absorbed this view of who should be in certain rooms, who should be the representatives when it comes to leadership, and it isn't all about talent. We throw around the word "professionalism" almost as a cover. So much of how we view professionalism is rooted in whiteness and class. I've been on the receiving end of this numerous times in my career, and it makes the pattern difficult to ignore.

WHAT'S REALLY GOING ON

Each of us should be mindful of this archetype because we can all contribute to what keeps it going. Often, people view this as something that only white people do to people of other races, only men do to women. We can't limit our thinking about who upholds certain cultural norms in the workplace. Just like the other archetypes, anyone of any age, race, gender, or background can lead in this way. Many people can say they make adjustments when they go to work, as that is simply part of having a job. I agree that being adaptable is a necessary skill. But there's an important difference between a person choosing to adjust and being required to suppress parts of who they are to be viewed as promotable or competent.

I've been on the receiving end of this from a diverse group of leaders, including other women, other Black people, other marginalized folks. Sometimes we police our own as harshly as others do—or even more so—in the workplace. It's important not to ignore this as if it's about someone else and could never be you. Sometimes this is simply about survival. If you've spent most of your career suppressing large parts of who you are, overworking, and outperforming others to make it to the top, perhaps you now expect everyone else to do the same. You don't want to lose your spot, so you make decisions based on what you think the dominant culture in the workplace would approve of. Not only do you not want to make the wrong choice, but you don't want to be replaced. What if the folks above your pay grade end up liking and respecting that very type of employee, that very type of woman, or—fill in the blank with any other group—what if they prefer that? Especially if you are the opposite?

You can become the very system that once frustrated and angered you. You were rewarded along the way for fitting in; sometimes you take pride in being that exception. But I wonder if shame pops up at times too. Over time, you develop a different definition of culture that's about optics and your own comfort; it's part of the game at work. It's OK to want to be comfortable for a change in life, but at what expense? You put so much value on things like being articulate, speaking with a certain tone, looking a certain way, and then use that against those around you. When people are confident, bold, or just communicate in a different way from you, you treat that difference as some sort of threat.

As mentioned before, anyone can be a Culture Enforcer, whether they are from a marginalized background or not. If you're not from a marginalized group, you're doing what we are all used to seeing, surrounding yourself with people who look like you and lead like you. You are upholding this idea of playing the game at work and rewarding those who do so, as well as those who assimilate into a specific way of being.

The fear here, like that of some other archetypes, is not being relevant anymore. There is a fear that the old way of being at work—phony, safe, similar—is going to be replaced by a new way of being that is more inclusive, bold, young, and authentic. You want things to remain the same, and people who give a vibe of not going along with the traditional ways of doing things will be pushed aside by Culture Enforcers like you. There's a sense of entitlement, too. If I had to sacrificc parts of who I really am to get here, I should be rewarded, as should those who are doing the same.

WHAT THEY WON'T TELL YOU

- "Sometimes it's a blessing to not be elevated in the cult-like spaces. It hurts at the time and feels personal—but it can be a gift to not be easily swayed into a culture you're not meant to fit into."
- "I'm introverted but a great worker and leader."
- "I (a single mom) recently did not get a promotion because the VP said, 'You're not able to travel, and it's a requirement of the job.' No opportunity to even see if I would be able to."
- "I can say I have been called aggressive for giving the same energy as a guy when I'm being direct while they called him assertive."
- "I lost myself and my skills listening to others tell me who and what I am and should do."
- "I'm neurodivergent and I had to understand that some folks just did not understand my processing and communication style. I also had to learn that some folks did not care, and they were intentional in that."
- "It's like they personally want to punish us. If you got it, help bring someone else up. We're more powerful together!"

BASED ON A TRUE STORY: CULTURE ENFORCER–MANAGED EMPLOYEE NO. 1

No matter what I do, I'll never be enough here. I'm looking at the people who've been moving up here, those who seem to be thriving here, and they are nothing like me. I've been pretending a bit, but I'm not that great at it, and I'm tired. Mentally and physically tired. There's no way for me to win. If I speak up, it's a problem; when I say nothing, that's also a problem. I have to be so careful with my tone, how I write emails—I'm under so much scrutiny. I feel like I'm becoming such a fraud; they want me to be so watered down. The way I dress now is just, ugh. If my friends and family saw how I act here, they would laugh. I'm here, but not really. I used to want to be a part of projects, go out after work with them, but I can't even do it now because everyone seems so phony, or they all just seem alike. I'm definitely looking for another job now.

BASED ON A TRUE STORY: CULTURE ENFORCER–MANAGED EMPLOYEE NO. 2

They really don't care about excellence here. Some of these people were where I am and made it, and you would think they would be different about who they gave opportunities to, but nope. They want people to code switch and be palatable like them. I'm not gonna be anyone's puppet or sell out; that's for sure. So much is a lie here. They say, "Oh, we want people to be themselves," but they just want you to be the version of yourself that's easiest to digest. They need to stop telling me to smile in these meetings—for what? I'm just supposed to smile for no reason? I'm not afraid to call things out, which is exactly what I'm about to start doing. What do I have to lose? I'm already going nowhere here. At least I can say what I think on my way out. It's true that people want you to shrink, but I'm not doing that.

HOW TO MAKE THE SHIFT FROM CULTURE ENFORCER TO CULTURE SUPPORTER

1. Culture Supporters start with self-awareness. There may be a bias, whether conscious or unconscious. You don't have to tell anyone; just acknowledge it within yourself so you can move forward. Be specific about what your bias is. Where do you think it comes from?
2. Break the cycle. At some point we have to stop treating other people the way we've been treated. You may be mad, but directing that energy toward people who have nothing to do with your past (or present) is unfair. What have you had to do to become accepted in your career? Have you ever had to suppress a part of who you are? How did it make you feel? It wasn't OK when it was done to you, and it's not OK for you to do it to someone else. If all your life you have had to fight, I'm so sorry, but it ends now.
3. Stop picking mini-me's to mentor. You are overlooking people who may challenge you, have a different vibe, and just make you uncomfortable. Try doing the opposite and select some of those people

to support and sponsor, not turn into you. This isn't about choosing people who are mean or off-putting; it's about seeing and selecting folks who make you uncomfortable because they are different. They don't have to share your leadership approach or style to be excellent at what they do and to have a place in your organization—either right next to you or far above you.

4. Redefine what leadership means to you. Make a list of what you think a leader looks, sounds, feels like. How does a leader behave? In another column, give the "why" behind each point on your list. It's not about being right or wrong; it's about exploring where your beliefs come from.
5. Start small. Identify someone who you don't think has the leadership presence you find acceptable. Give them a small project to take the lead on, let them run a meeting, and see how they do. Take note of how you feel about the way they do things. Make sure you offer them the same level of support, resources and guidance you would offer to one of your favorites. Is it so terrible because they are different? How does this truly impact you, the team, or the company?
6. Approach interviews in a new way. Bias starts early, during résumé reviews and first impressions. When you speak with candidates, including staff ready for promotions, don't immediately focus on polish, style, or "fit." Think about how they may add

something unique to the existing team due to their skills, experience, and background.

7. It's OK to question your gut. Sometimes your gut feeling could be wrong. If you feel more comfortable with one person over another, whether during a hiring process or within your team, ask yourself some questions. What makes me more comfortable with certain people? What would be different if I looked for shared values instead of a shared background and way of thinking? What are the values we have as a team, and how do I evaluate where people align, if at all?

8

The Toxic Optimist / Pretender

IS THIS YOU?

- ☐ I believe people can't handle the truth.
- ☐ The workplace isn't a space for too much emotion, especially negative emotion.
- ☐ If I tell people the truth, they will lose confidence in me.
- ☐ When I hear feedback, it often sounds like people are complaining.
- ☐ I shouldn't have to explain everything; people should be able to read between the lines.
- ☐ Withholding information is my way of protecting my staff so they can just focus on their jobs.
- ☐ I avoid talking about challenges with my staff for as long as possible.

- ☐ When things are clearly not going well, my go-to phrase is "Let's stay positive."
- ☐ Things could be worse; I tell people that all the time.
- ☐ Sometimes I frame unreasonable workloads as "stretch opportunities."

8–10 STATEMENTS THAT APPLY

High alignment: You strongly reflect this archetype. These behaviors show up often and impact your leadership presence and team dynamics.

4–7 STATEMENTS THAT APPLY

Moderate alignment: Some tendencies are present for you. You may slip into this archetype when you feel stressed by a specific event or person. With awareness, you can adjust and shift away from this energy.

0–3 STATEMENTS THAT APPLY

Low alignment: This archetype isn't dominant in your leadership style. Still, stay aware of these behaviors creeping in under pressure.

PATTERN RECOGNITION

As a Toxic Optimist / Pretender, you aren't always intentionally withholding the truth outright, which can make you particularly frustrating. In some cases, you truly believe you are helping people by not telling them much. You also believe you're helping yourself stay sane, stay positive, and appear to have it together. You'll say things like "We got this," "We're doing so well," and "Don't worry." These phrases can be harmless and appropriate if they are actually true. When they aren't true, this is a big problem. You avoid telling your staff much about what's happening; instead, you focus on using the right words and putting on the right face to make them feel comfortable in the midst of disaster. It doesn't work past a short period of time because eventually, people believe what they see and feel, not what is simply presented—especially if it's in direct opposition with their reality. You try to motivate and uplift your staff during the worst of times and never give a direct answer to a question. You either don't know the answer and refuse to say that, or you do know but don't want to tell your staff.

Everything is about optics for Toxic Optimists. You think you have the power to shift other people's reality with a wink and a smile. If you respected your staff, you would give them the opportunity to hear hard news and handle real data. People feel like their power to decide what to do for themselves is taken away because they never have accurate or enough information.

It's one thing to have a single manager like this, but some companies operate this way. You'll see staff basically split into two groups: those who pretend, just like management, and work hard to perform as if everything is OK and exciting when it isn't; and those who question things, advocate for themselves and others, and are viewed as difficult and not team players. When the company culture is one of toxic optimism or positivity, the crash (layoffs, for example) feels extra harsh because staff realize they were being lied to the whole time—something that can change you forever.

MY TOXIC-OPTIMIST STORY

A manager once told me to never let my staff know what's going on or how I'm feeling. That made me nervous because it was so different from my own beliefs. I started to see that we were perhaps a mismatch. This was said to me within the first two weeks of my new role, and I was already overwhelmed with so much. Things weren't very organized in the company, there was very little training and support from my new boss, and I was greeted on day one by a lovely yet disgruntled staff. I understood their sentiment—that it's important not to cause your staff to panic—but I also am a pretty transparent person.

There were a number of things not going well behind the scenes, and my boss would always show up as if things were easy breezy, even though it was very obvious that things weren't OK. Everyone could see it, and that caused a ton of chatter, which I thought was becoming more and more of a problem. My manager didn't appear stronger or in control, which is probably what they believed and intended. Since they didn't address or explain anything, they appeared sinister, delusional, disrespectful, and some people resented them for it. I don't think that's an accurate description of who they were, but that's how they appeared. Personally, I see nothing wrong with letting staff know the real numbers or the concerns, because in some instances, this information can motivate, encourage, or simply explain why certain things are happening. I think folks forget that we're all adults and are reasonable when we get things like truth and context. Instead of treating staff like adults, Toxic Optimists withhold information and grin through it all until it becomes impossible for them to keep doing so.

What frustrated me most was my former boss never allowed people to really see them and wanted me to mirror their lack of authenticity, which is a top value for me. It angered me, maybe more than it should have, but our values are who we are. So, I had someone trying to coach me to become someone I am not. I did allow my staff to see various parts of me, not because I wanted to be liked, but because it was easier and more natural for me to just be transparent, for better or for worse. My staff saw that I could handle challenges but also saw that I had struggles and didn't know it all. I let them know that I understood I wasn't the only leader in the room and that I could learn from them. We could learn from each other. This helped because they sometimes used their own creativity to solve problems in moments when I was stuck or too overwhelmed with being the manager to do so. This is how you can empower a team and motivate people whose decision to stay or resign rests on the level of respect they have for you as a leader.

WHAT'S REALLY GOING ON

If you resonate even moderately with this leadership style, it's easy to see why. Appearing weak is the last thing some people want, especially if you worked really hard to get to where you are, overcame a ton of obstacles, have a history of doing well, or come from a historically marginalized background. You may have come across people who question whether you're qualified or deserving of your position and level of pay. Why show any sign of how rough things are, which would just validate someone's past or present critique or view that you couldn't cut it? That energy of fear and avoidance can pop up here, and you'll start creating scenarios. You may think about being honest and upfront but talk yourself out of it because you don't want to let people know you were wrong. Maybe you try to convince yourself that things really aren't that bad and that you can turn it around before the worst happens. If this is the case, then showing emotion, admitting a mistake, or appearing like you aren't in total control is unnecessary, right? You put so much pressure on yourself, but you may have been raised that way or had a really bad experience at work or even school along the way.

If you're someone who is a people pleaser, you may live here too. You want to come off as positive and can become obsessed with bringing good vibes. Every day, people go to work in environments where any level of dissent, any hard question, would cause a pearl clutch. The only voices allowed to be heard are those that speak only of the bright side—those willing and ready to "sell" whatever leadership comes up with. In these spaces, of course people will refrain from being honest and real when difficulties or messes are brewing behind the scenes. That can cause you to lose your job, so in order to survive, you'll adopt the same fake behavior as the leadership you report to. You see that the truth tellers are punished either via lack of promotions or being pulled into meetings to "watch your tone." When it all comes crashing down, it's going to be bad for everyone, especially those who played these roles and played in everyone's face. This is a choice.

The gaslighting is really what causes people who report to you to lose it. The way you repeatedly tell people that what they are seeing and experiencing isn't real is frustrating. Where did you learn to do this? Somewhere along the way, at home or early in your career, you were trained to perform this way. Whatever is happening that is wrong or uncomfortable, you believe you have to grin and bear it. A lot of people say that in their families, they didn't talk about problems. This doesn't mean you'll end up being a Toxic Optimist at work, but it can give some insight into why it's so discomforting for you to just tell people when things aren't OK.

The idealists who are in a stressful space have to be extra careful here. As someone who has worked in several nonprofit organizations, I find that the toxic optimism and pretending can feel like they are at crisis levels within these organizations. You will feel like you're losing your mind. I'm an idealist and a trained coach—the ways I've had to question and reject parts of my training are real. There have been instances when I've had to pause and accept that there's nothing I can say to someone on the receiving end of racism, sexism, ableism, that's going to change what they're going through. People working in a burnout culture don't want you to gloss over their stress and health issues by telling them how this experience will be a good résumé builder. What's happening to people is real, and they should be heard. You don't always have to look for the bright side, but let's say you want to stick to that because it's a personal value. That's fine—for you. The issue is when you project your way of thinking onto others. Your go-to responses don't always need to be that there's something to be learned, that there's a reason for everything, that we all are doing exactly what we should, no matter how hard—it's exhausting! People don't want or need to hear that every time things are hard. Some systems and environments are harmful; it's OK to acknowledge that and let people be.

What is comforting to you may feel highly disrespectful to others, not because they are negative, but because they are able to be real in moments when you are willing to perform. Leadership, to you, is cheerleading. Who can be the most upbeat, the most positive, the most performative. That isn't leadership, especially when people around you are truly struggling. You are not weak for wanting to bring some reality to your team.

WHAT THEY WON'T TELL YOU

- "My employer laid off 50 percent of the staff yesterday. Fear and panic set in. Morale was already low . . . I'm a team lead and often find myself filling in and helping because I want to take some of the burden off my boss. Meanwhile the owners of this company are busy making YouTube videos about their personal life."
- "The amount of mental stress a toxic workplace takes on you is astounding."
- "I gained thirty pounds in two toxic years at my last job. 'Today was stressful,' I deserve a little sweet treat. I was self-soothing with food."

BASED ON A TRUE STORY: TOXIC OPTIMIST–MANAGED EMPLOYEE NO. 1

Every day feels surreal. It's like watching a documentary where a person is describing something terrible that has happened, but they have a smile on their face. The words coming out of their mouth and the scene unfolding don't match. It starts to become scary over time. The last few times I brought up a real issue with how things are being done here, I got a weird response. It was as if I had completely made up my experience! They just glossed over it so calmly and acted like everything was OK. All they talked about was the bright side, and it's never really bright. I walked away feeling like I'm the problem. I'm on my own. My colleagues are always upbeat in the Zoom chats and appear to be OK with everything. When we go into those breakout rooms, they sound more like me. Everything and everyone here is so fake. Or just scared, like me. I don't even care anymore about how we're doing. My manager is always smiling and isn't concerned, so why should I be?

BASED ON A TRUE STORY: TOXIC OPTIMIST-MANAGED EMPLOYEE NO. 2

They're insulting my intelligence. There's no way my manager is so secure and so strong in the middle of all this mess. Why can't they just address it? Why do I have to look like Debbie Downer just for acknowledging real challenges? I'm not going to keep holding it in during these meetings; I just have to say what I think and what I'm seeing. I'm not the one who needs an attitude adjustment or needs to be more positive; they need to be real. I'm tired of the gaslighting and these scary-looking smiles. Maybe if they just tell us what the problems are, we can help solve them. The safest thing for me to do is keep to myself. I can't absorb this phony energy;

I have to stay true to who I am. They'll get the bare minimum from me, even though I know they need more.

HOW TO MAKE THE SHIFT FROM PRETENDER TO TRUTH TELLER

1. Get real with yourself privately about what isn't going well for you in your role. You can start by writing about this in a journal or by sharing it with someone else, like a therapist, coach, mentor, or friend. Pretending within yourself makes it easy to pretend with others, and it's harmful in both instances. Things are falling apart! It happens; just acknowledge that things aren't easy, and sometimes the pressure put on you and others is unfair.
2. Share some of how you are feeling with your staff. Talking about pain or hardship doesn't create more of it. It can feel a bit risky to be vulnerable, but I think there are more pros than cons. Even in the workplace, you will find there do exist people who are understanding and eager to help. Not just for your benefit, but for theirs as well. Everyone doesn't struggle with hardship in the way that you do. I'm not suggesting you overshare and burden your staff with all your emotions, but instead of lying with a smile, try telling the truth, with some hope mixed in. This may go against a lot of what you believe and have been taught, but there are people who will feel relief to hear you speak to the challenges of your work environment. You don't have to bad-mouth the company leaders or be

doom and gloom. There is room for hope in many situations, especially when you release the burden from yourself and invite other people to be a part of solving problems. Managers struggle and make mistakes too, and people should know that's a normal part of the job.

3. Create spaces for staff to share their experience without judgment and retaliation. Yeah, this might feel like another difficult step. If you've already shared your own struggles, it can help people feel more comfortable opening up (though not completely). Maybe you ask a question in 1:1s about what isn't going well. Maybe there's a shared document where people can post questions or speak to a specific frustration they would like help moving past in their work. You may have an open forum with anonymous info written on pieces of paper and placed in a box. I've done this, and it wasn't as scary as I thought, but yes, people did name an issue or two with me. They were polite about it, but I got the point and they were right about what they said. This can help tune you into how people feel and what they're struggling with, and it will let your staff know they aren't alone or crazy for sharing some similar challenges. Will you feel attacked? Maybe. Is that what's most important? No.
4. Know your limits. It's not your job to make everyone feel good; it's your job to let people know the truth and then let them decide what they do with that information. How good people feel at work

about anything is influenced by you, but we are all ultimately responsible for our feelings.

5. Validate how people feel. You don't have to agree with what they think or how they feel, but a simple acknowledgment makes people feel seen, like letting someone know "This is a lot of work being put on you at the last minute, and it's understandable that you feel overwhelmed. We have a big goal to serve ten thousand more customers by the end of the year, so this is something we are doing to try to get to that number." You're not agreeing with them nor releasing any deep, dark secrets.
6. Become more curious. This is Coaching 101, and as a manager, part of your job is to coach. Coaches always ask questions first. When people share a frustration or point out something related to the work or your leadership, ask open-ended questions to gain more understanding instead of getting defensive. If someone says, "I'm overwhelmed," don't respond with statements about how everyone else seems to be fine, talk about how close the team is to their goal, or question their work ethic. Instead, try asking, "How long have you been feeling overwhelmed?," "How much time are you giving to certain projects?," and so on. Try to understand what's going on and listen, versus trying to explain away or dismiss everything.
7. Avoid being a master of deflection. You know how to avoid direct people and difficult conversations because they make you uncomfortable at times.

Practice telling people "I don't know everything that's happening, but here's what I do know," and be honest. When people come to you with an issue, it's OK to pause and gather your thoughts so you can give a proper response, which will be different from what you're used to doing. You're not going to engage in "spin"—"This is a great opportunity for you!"—and you're not going to minimize it. Instead, you'll ask the kind of questions that not just a coach but also a collaborator would ask. "Let's figure this out together" will get you far more respect than making people feel like what they're experiencing isn't real.

9

Breaking the Patterns

THE LEADERSHIP THAT STAYS WITH YOU

- “I want a manager to be a team player and not take credit for others’ work. A manager that will stand up for their team. A manager that will listen.”
- “Teach what they know to those who want to learn.”
- “Great managers create an environment of working as a team, not pit the employees against each other.”
- “I’d like a manager who asks my opinion and listens when I give it. I don’t need to be agreed with, but I do need to be heard.”
- “Good managers are happy but sad to see their developed employees spread their wings and leave the nest for a promotion because of their growth.”

Great leadership feels light, connected, and inspiring. When I think about my favorite managers, and the managers my colleagues and clients have loved, they share similar qualities and behave in similar ways. I don't know for a fact that they were whole, but they seemed to lead with more ease than the managers who give people the hardest time.

They were able to see the value in each and every person on their team and wanted everyone else to know. These managers don't discourage their staff and don't pick at the things they do. Even when they know ideas aren't perfect, they coach people by asking questions to help them think things through.

They're confident that their staff will do well, and even if they don't, they'll learn something from it, and that's enough for them. Their feedback isn't always positive or exactly what people want to hear, but it's well received because it's specific and always about work. They never avoid conversations; instead, they initiate them.

We love managers who don't glorify overwork. I had a manager contact me to tell me I hadn't taken much time off that year and encourage me to take more. They are the ones who may work late into the evening and on their off days, but they don't feel the need to tell us that. There's an understanding that not everyone has to work in the same way.

Great leadership feels safe. These leaders know how to create a space where people know they won't be judged. It is nice not to have to work so hard to withhold parts of yourself at work, which is something so many people tell me they have to do. To be able to go to work each day and not have to pretend to be less intelligent, less capable, less efficient because someone who is supposed to be your leader might be bothered by that, or take advantage of that, is a beautiful thing.

DESIGN YOUR OWN LEADERSHIP

What's so great about leadership is that we can design it for ourselves. We have the power to choose, and that power is everything. Leadership doesn't have to look any specific way, so we can create our own style, vibe, energy—whatever you want to call it—and just be that. It's like going into the kitchen and whipping up a dish in your own way, even after someone gives you their recipe. People can still enjoy your version of that recipe. Let's approach leadership that way.

You've seen various leadership failures in this book that may resonate with you. Now, you'll design your own approach based on how you want to feel, the vibe you want to bring to people around you, and the type of actions you want to take in your career.

We're going to design with our values as the foundation, add what we want, and subtract what doesn't work for us anymore. We'll be able to acknowledge our challenges and plan how we'll handle them when they pop up. If you want to lead with a more intentional vibe, a lot of the fear and self-doubt will have to go. We'll need to work on becoming whole, which includes being confident and improving your self-worth.

Before we start designing our unique leadership approach, we need to remove what blocks us. A lot of the time, we look at others as being in our way. Our family, friends, and—in the case of managers—often our staff or leaders. You won't get much done here by way of making a change if you don't identify what's in the way and remove it.

FIND YOUR FEAR

Most of us have something we fear. Fear itself isn't terrible—it's normal. It's our inability to name and push through our fears that can cause us to become a nightmare for the people around us. It's worth putting in the time to figure out and own if you want to make any real, consistent change.

Fear is a common thread running through every archetype in this book. Whether you're a new manager or a more seasoned one, it can pop up at times, even when you have the best intentions. It's like knowing what healthy foods we're supposed to choose, but when stress hits, we end up in the unhealthy part of the grocery store.

Take the archetype(s) you resonate with, along with the shifts outlined at the end of each chapter, and start planning! The following are some reminders of common fears associated with the archetypes. (This isn't meant to be an all-inclusive list.)

THE MICROMANAGER / CONTROL FREAK

- Fear of being blamed when things aren't perfect
- Fear of being exposed as incompetent

THE ABSENTEE MANAGER / GHOST

- Fear of being exposed for not knowing what's going on
- Fear of conflict or uncomfortable conversations

THE SPOTLIGHT SEEKER / CREDIT STEALER

- Fear of other people being recognized over you
- Fear of being invisible

THE GATEKEEPER / BLOCKER

- Fear of being outshined
- Fear of losing control over access

THE BURNOUT CREATOR / MARTYR

- Fear of appearing lazy or weak
- Fear that others will succeed without "suffering"

THE CULTURE ENFORCER / MOLD MAKER

- Fear of difference
- Fear of being blamed if things go wrong

THE TOXIC OPTIMIST / PRETENDER

- Fear that honesty will lower morale
- Fear of discomfort, or any negative emotion

REMOVE YOUR LEADERSHIP BLOCKS

Use these questions to identify leadership blocks you need to remove. I've included sample answers following the questions.

The archetype(s) I resonate the most with is/are:

My biggest fear as a manager is:

I believe I have this fear because (if you don't know exactly, make your best guess!):

Carrying this fear has caused me to do the following as a manager:

Other emotions I have felt connected to this fear:

Instead of fear, I'd like to feel:

Here's what would be different about the way I lead if fear and other related emotions weren't in the way:

Here's an example of how someone who identifies as being a Micromanager might answer these questions.

The archetype(s) I resonate the most with is/are: Micromanager

My biggest fear as a manager is: Being viewed as incompetent

I believe I have this fear because: A mentor shared with me that you have to ensure they need you at work so you don't get laid off.

Carrying this fear has caused me to do the following as a manager: I redo work, stay late, worry I'll get blamed for mistakes.

Other emotions I have felt connected to this fear: Anxiety, exhaustion

Instead of fear, I'd like to feel: Trust

Here's what would be different about the way I lead if fear and other related emotions weren't in the way: I'd delegate without hovering.

BUILD YOUR LEADERSHIP FOUNDATION

Now that you see how fear has gotten in your way and what you want to feel instead, let's get clear on a fresh foundation on which to build this new leadership energy. Our values are our foundation. Assess and develop your list of core, nonnegotiable values. If you don't know what's nonnegotiable, what's most important to you, you will always feel unsteady. You'll just keep adjusting to what others want, even when it's not in alignment with who you are. Something what happens in management is you get caught up as the face and voice of policies and a culture you don't even believe in. When you are firm in what you believe, this won't feel as difficult to navigate.

The quickest way to identify your core values is to just think about periods in your life when you were happy and felt accomplished and at ease.

- What was going on at the time?
- What values were you living true to that led to you feeling so happy?

Another way to get an idea of your values is to look at your friends, family members, public figures, and leaders from your past and present.

- What qualities do they have that you admire?

Identify those values and then pull them together into a simple statement you can lead from.

As a leader, I value ________, ________, and ________. I bring ____________________, and I make decisions that reflect ______________________________ __________________.

Here's an example of what my value statement might be:

As a leader, I value autonomy, transparency, and advocacy. I bring honesty and courage, and I make decisions that reflect my commitment to truth, fairness, and people's growth, including my own.

I had to throw that last bit in there, because I want to help you but also help myself at the same time!

Now do this for yourself, even if you have to create multiple versions. You can also do this with your peers or your staff.

CREATE A VALUES-BASED ACTION PLAN

The last thing I'll say here is don't just talk about it, be about it. One of my biggest pet peeves with companies is that they talk a good game about values and make sure they are highlighted everywhere. The audacity comes in, though, when you work there and see that those values don't mean much in reality. The actions from the top down don't align. This is frustrating and causes resentment when you start to see how fraudulent things feel. It's not enough to say what you stand for; you have to actually live and work true to those values. They're not supposed to be an afterthought; they're supposed to be a part of the culture every day.

Write down each of the values you listed in your value statement.

Under each value, list three actions you can take to live those values as a manager.

Fear was shaping you as a leader up until now, and your values are taking you to where you want to go next. Leading from values will make you whole again, or for the first time. Let's talk about what wholeness as a leader means.

BECOME WHOLE AS A LEADER

What's going to make you feel at your best as a leader is becoming whole. A whole person has a healthy level of self-esteem and confidence. It sounds simple, but many people don't have both; they have one, or neither. If you have both, you're a whole leader, and you won't resonate strongly with any of the archetypes mentioned in this book. You'll go to work whole; you'll lead this way. If you're committed to working to build this back up or develop it for the first time, let's do it. You'll be able to handle the challenges that come your way, and you'll also model this for your staff, who should also try to become whole as employees.

Confident people know what they can do. They have a strong belief in their own abilities and trust their own judgment. They're willing to take action in instances where other people are not. They know how to advocate for themselves and stand in their truth. When it comes to people with high self-esteem, they don't need external validation to feel worthy. They know that, regardless of what happens, regardless of how many times they mess up, and regardless of what anyone says, they are still valuable. They know they aren't perfect, but they know they are worthy. Becoming whole isn't about being perfect or never having a bad day or cursing someone out in your head. It's about being steady. You can handle things. You get rejected; you get back up. There's an opportunity and you're interested; you go for it. There's a difficult conversation to be had; you set it up. Tough feedback is given to you; you listen, take what you need to learn, and don't hold a grudge against the person who gave it to you.

BUILD CONFIDENCE AND SELF-WORTH

GET RID OF PRAISE I want you to stop outsourcing your self-worth. Feeling valuable and good about yourself will never come from someone else. Nobody can give you that. Your leadership won't make you valuable, nor will your staff. So, get rid of the need for praise. I know it helps us feel good, but if you remove all the praise, all the promotions, if you remove the things that people say about you—what do you think about yourself?

SPEAK KINDLY TO YOURSELF Work on speaking to yourself in a different way. One thing that stands out in my coaching sessions is how unbelievably hard y'all are on yourselves! No matter how accomplished and talented you are, it is so easy for people to tell me what they do wrong, where they messed up. When I ask people to tell me what they're proud of, what their strengths are, they struggle way more than they should to answer those questions. I'm hard on myself too, so don't think I view myself as high and mighty. And honestly, every day is hard for a lot of people, going to work in places that are very demanding, ruthless, and unsafe. I think it's important for you to affirm yourself more often. You do have value regardless of how that presentation went. You are worthy despite that error your team made. You have to know that despite what's happening around you, you have value. You don't need to be the most liked person, the most praised person; you don't need to be the smartest person in the room to have value.

BUILD BOUNDARIES Stop being so available to everyone all the time. Absentee Managers, maybe skip this one, or just learn a bit about balance! Whole people are not always available to everybody. They prioritize how they spend their time and with whom. Have you ever come across people who you can't just easily access with nonsense? They know how to be there for others when truly needed, but everyone doesn't get to drain them. Some of you, especially the Micromanagers and Burnout Creators, are always trying to help this person and that person and be here and there. By the end of the day, week, and so on, there's nothing left! A whole person prioritizes their well-being because they know that's healthy. They understand that they're not always agreeable. They might disagree; they're not easy to manipulate. If the thought of this makes you uncomfortable, that makes sense. Some of you have employees like that and you push them away because they are so different from you. But you can learn so much from them and have a much stronger team.

AFFIRM WHOLENESS

There's a saying I grew up with: "Real recognizes real." Well, "whole recognizes whole." When I talk about becoming whole, it's usually directed toward people like the ones on your staff—those who internalize poor leadership as something wrong with themselves. When you read the employee voice number 1 in the archetype chapters, you'll find examples of how people take in what you're doing wrong, blame themselves, or lose whatever self-esteem they had to begin with. They are responding to your energy with a similar energy, creating a back-and-forth struggle and often fostering a toxic work environment. When you become whole, you think differently, feel differently, and act differently. You're modeling healthy leadership, and others on your team are safe being whole right along with you. They're not a threat to you anymore; you're like minded.

How are we supposed to get whole, especially in these workplaces that can feel like they are setting us up to be anything but that? A good first step toward becoming whole is to know who you are, independent of any of the other things going on around you. So, who are you? Not simply your job title and salary, which tell me what you do and what you have. This is a question about values, which we have covered. You should be able to express that value statement anytime, anyplace. That's a quick, direct overview of who you are.

Let's make this idea of wholeness clearer for you. I like affirmations, so let's do this affirmation-style. You can, but don't have to, put this on Post-it notes around your home or declare it to the world; this is for you to know as a reminder. Things get shaky. No matter what we know about leadership and confidence, we don't know what each workday will bring. People act like fools; they question us; they test us. This doesn't mean we fall apart, because we are always working on being solid.

So, fill in the following Wholeness Affirmation with a unique reminder for yourself:

I'm becoming a leader who ________________________ ____________.

I trust that I can lead with ______________________ instead of fear.

Even when things get uncomfortable, I'll go right back to ______________________________.

Here's what my Wholeness Affirmation might look like:

I'm becoming a leader who doesn't shrink, perform, or apologize for being clear.

I trust that I can lead with honesty instead of fear.

Even when things get uncomfortable, I'll go right back to my values and know that I've figured things out before and can do that again.

ANYONE CAN BECOME A GOOD MANAGER

This is a book to give you hope. Resonating with these archetypes at a medium to high level is normal for many and not the end of the world. Just as I was able to grow out of being an Absentee Manager, you can grow out of being a Micromanager. You can stop being a Gatekeeper. You can become less biased. You can be optimistic, but real. You don't have to hover over people, and you don't need to burn yourself out in the process.

This isn't a book about how you will always be; it's a chance to see where you are right now and the possibilities available if, tomorrow, you want to try something different. You have identified your fears and can get started pushing through them. You can build a new foundation on your non-negotiable values. You can become whole and the type of leader who makes a positive impact on everyone around you.

ACKNOWLEDGMENTS

My forever bestie and favorite Leo, Nya. You were my number one motivator in putting this out into the world. I hope you'll think this is cool someday.

To my mom, also a writer, I'm so thankful you passed down a love of reading and writing to me. You tried your best to prepare me for the workplace; I just didn't listen!

To my dad for always encouraging me to build something of my own.

To my agent, Natalie Lakosil, who may be the most patient person I've ever met. Thank you for giving me a chance and helping me to fulfill a lifelong dream.

To Neal Maillet, my champion! You encouraged me to be me and let me know that my voice is OK. I'll never forget how you had my back during this process.

To Jeevan Sivasubramaniam, your wise words and advice were always noted. I replay in my mind a number of things you've said, and that has helped me to feel confident about what I put together here.

To the entire Berrett-Koehler team, working with you on all parts of this so far has been a great chance to learn so much about publishing and see how talented you are at what you do. I will never look at a book in the same way again.

To Britt, your thoughtful and respectful feedback shaped this book in a big way. Thank you.

To my social media community, over 130,000 of you, thank you. I hope I have conveyed all the emotions you have shared with me in comments, emails, and direct messages over the last four years. This book is so special because it comes from you.

I'm grateful to clients, family, and friends who have trusted me with your experiences. While no individual stories are shared here, you've helped me to see what is needed and what is possible.

I've been fortunate to have worked with and for some of the smartest, most dedicated, selfless people throughout my career. Thank you for being a model of great leadership.

To my closest friends and extended family, I appreciate having you there to confide in for many years and am glad we could support each other through all the ups and downs of our careers.

Dr. C, Tyisha, Amenze, Jackie, Nikki, Trevor, and Cairo: Thank you for lots of love and for letting me practice my coaching on you—whether you wanted it or not. I'm most thankful for the moments over the years when we could eat, compete, and be merry.

RECOMMENDED READING AND RESOURCES

Cain, Susan. *Quiet: The Power of Introverts in a World That Can't Stop Talking.* The Crown Publishing Group, 2013.

Energy Leadership Index (ELI). A leadership assessment administered by certified coaches through Institute for Professional Excellence in Coaching. https://www.energyleadership.com/assessment.

Fuller, Pamela, Mark Murphy, and Anne Chow. *The Leader's Guide to Unconscious Bias: How To Reframe Bias, Cultivate Connection, and Create High-Performing Teams.* Simon & Schuster, 2023.

Harts, Minda. *The Memo: What Women of Color Need to Know to Secure a Seat at the Table.* Seal Press, 2020.

Hersey, Tricia. *Rest Is Resistance: Free Yourself from Grind Culture and Reclaim Your Life.* Little, Brown Spark, 2022.

Schneider, Bruce D. *Energy Leadership: Transforming Your Workplace and Your Life from the Core.* Wiley, 2007.

Tawwab, Nedra Glover. *Set Boundaries, Find Peace: A Guide to Reclaiming Yourself.* Tarcher, 2021.

INDEX

F

M

R

S

T

U

V

W

Y

ABOUT THE AUTHOR

TANYA UYIGUE is a workplace strategist, writer, speaker, and content creator focused on leadership behavior and employee experience. She has spent over fifteen years designing and leading career development programs across local and national organizations, bringing a human-centered lens to conversations about voice, power, and management.

Trained as a professional coach through the Institute for Professional Excellence in Coaching (iPEC), Tanya has worked as a career coach and leadership adviser, drawing on real workplace experience and the stories of professionals navigating work every day. She holds a bachelor's degree in speech communication from the University of Illinois at Urbana-Champaign. Her work has been shared by Girlboss and Lean In and has appeared in *Bustle*, *Crain's Chicago Business*, and WGN-TV. She lives in Chicago with her family.

Berrett-Koehler

PUBLISHERS

Dear Reader,

Welcome to the Berrett-Koehler Community—a global network of changemakers creating positive impact in their lives, organizations, and communities.

Our Mission: Connecting People and Ideas to Create a World That Works for All

We believe transformation is possible. While outdated paradigms of self-interest, exclusion, and hierarchy continue to hold back our communities and organizations, we know that change can happen. That's why we connect people with actionable ideas from leading experts who are already creating the solutions we need.

The BK Way

We're an independent publisher that practices what we publish. Our books, digital resources, and community offerings provide practical pathways for building more just, equitable, and sustainable organizations and lives. Whether you're transforming your workplace, community, or personal practices, our publications meet you where you are with tools that work.

But we don't just talk about positive change—we live it. Through "The BK Way," we put stewardship and purpose before profit. As a benefit corporation, we're legally committed to benefiting all our stakeholders: authors, readers, employees, communities, and the environment.

As our gift to you, claim your free bestselling ebook at bkconnection.com/welcome. You'll also receive fresh leadership insights delivered to your inbox from bkconnection.com/blogs/the-bk-exchange.

You Make the Difference

We're grateful to our readers, authors, and community members, who bring our mission to life every day. Your stories of transformation inspire us and show others what's possible.

Share how BK publications are making a difference in your world at bkconnection.com/impact.

Your friends at Berrett-Koehler

Join the Berrett-Koehler Community

Are you passionate about supporting independent publishing and reading diverse voices and perspectives? Join the BK Community Membership Program and become a part of a vibrant literary community. To support mission-based publishing while saving up to 30 percent on all books and attending exclusive events, visit ideas.bkconnection.com/bkcommunity-join to learn more and become a member.

FSC www.fsc.org
MIX
Paper | Supporting responsible forestry
FSC® C005010